Creating Web Sites that WOW!

Everything you need to set-up a stunning Internet site

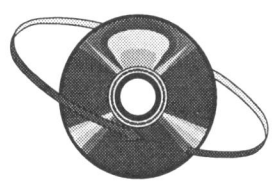

Mark Neely and Sarina Kreitmeier

NET-WORKS

PO BOX 200
Harrogate
HG1 2YR
England

www.net-works.co.uk
Email: sales@net-works.co.uk
Fax: +44 (0) 1423 526035

Net.Works is an imprint of Take That Ltd

ISBN: 1-873668-27-9

Text Copyright © 2000 Infolution Pty Ltd.
Design & Layout Copyright © 2000 Take That Ltd

Contents

Change of Address

When you try to access some of the sites recommended in this book you may come across the dreaded "file not found" screen or a similar message indicating the site is no longer located at the given address.

This isn't because we have given you the wrong address or mistyped it (though that may have happened, because we are only human!) but because the World Wide Web is in a constant stage of flux. Every day pages are being created, but also others disappear. Perhaps a company or person has a page on a certain ISP's computer, but they found a cheaper way to access the World Wide Web and changed ISP. So they have to take their page with them and load it onto another computer.

However there are a few tricks that you can try to locate the information you are after (assuming you have already checked that you've typed the address exactly as given):

- Try changing the file name extension from *.htm to *.html and visa versa.
- Add or subtract the www at the beginning of the page address.
- Play around with the capitalisation of the address, but remember that host names are not case sensitive.
- Remove the last part of the file name so that you are just left with the host name. You can then follow links on the site to try and find the page that you require.

If all else fails take a few key words from the page you are trying to find and go to a search engine. Even if this still does not find the site that you require you will at least find similar sites and perhaps still get the information you are after.

Introduction

Why Create a Website?

Do you remember the day you first used the Web? It's not exactly on a par with your first kiss, twenty-first birthday or wedding, but a lot of people recall that being on the Web was quite liberating.

Liberating? Well, yes. If you're like most people, you probably spent the first few hours flitting from website to website - not paying too much attention to what you saw, just marvelling at how easy it all was. Once you got the hang of the buttons and hyperlinks, you were off in search of information about your favourite hobby, musician, sports team or whatever took your fancy at the time.

It was liberating to be in a position to access information on demand. Instead of picking up the paper and reading what some anonymous editor had selected as the day's news, or turning on the TV and passively watching a program, you were free to seek out the information, news and entertainment you wanted!

Once the initial giddy excitement dies down a little, you start to become a little cynical. You encounter a few websites that are decidedly amateurish, or which contain dated or even incorrect information. "I could do much better," you think to yourself.

Well, you could, that is, if you just knew where to start!

Your First Website

There are many reasons for wanting to create a website. Some of the more obvious relate to the enormous profits analysts predict will be - and are being - made from the online consumer market.

But not everyone uses the Web for business. Many people use their website for non-profit or entirely personal reasons. For example, some use their website to publish poems, stories and novels they have written and want to share with the world. Others use their website as a public diary, noting on it their life's events. Families have been known to create Web-based photo albums so that relatives around the world can watch the children grow up.

Many personal websites are used to collect and distribute jokes and other humorous items. Other sites are composed of an index of sites that relate to a specific topic, such as a favourite band, sport or actor. There are also more practical uses for the Web. For example, many job-hunters create websites that contain a personal résumé, to which they can point potential employers. Others use their sites to post timetables for everything from their high school basket-ball team's game schedule to the national football competition league table.

The fact that you're reading this book (or skimming through it in a bookstore) means that you probably already have a reason for wanting to stake out your own piece of Web turf.

About Websites

There is more to creating a website than simply throwing together a few pictures and some text. There are marketing issues to be considered (which apply even if yours is a purely personal site), such as who you want to visit your site, and how you plan to attract them. What will they expect to find when they get there?

In addition there are technical issues to be considered. Will your website cater for any user, or only those with the latest in Web technology? Will your site be bandwidth-friendly, or will users require a high-speed Internet connection to access all you offer? And there are also design issues to consider. How will users navigate around the site? Do you want or need a logo so visitors can identify you as the owner of the site? What colours and fonts should you use? Will each section of your site have a consistent look, or will they be designed independently?

Finally, it is important at the outset to understand why you want a website, as this will determine exactly how much time, money, effort and sweat you are prepared to invest in creating and maintaining your website.

Why This Book?

When we initially conceived the idea for this book, we surveyed existing Web design titles, and found that - as a rule - they tended to focus only on a single aspect of Web design. For instance, some books tended to look at the Web from a graphic design perspective, teaching readers how to make pretty Web graphics.

Others examined only the technological perspective, explaining how to use the latest tools to create groovy interactive websites. And still others took a document-layout viewpoint, suggesting which fonts, colours and layout to use to maximise readability. Few books addressed all these issues, and even fewer were written for those putting together their first website.

In preparing this book, we were determined to present a more holistic overview of website creation. In doing so, we spent almost as much time deciding what to leave out as deciding what to include. For instance, while there are some excellent graphic-design packages available (such as Adobe PageMaker), we realised that these were beyond the budget of most users. Instead, we elected to focus on free or shareware packages. Similarly, while there are some really nifty Web authoring programs, we preferred those that were available in demo versions (so users could "try-before-you-buy") and those that were reasonably priced. We also felt it was important that our readers gained a broad understanding of the basics of good website design, rather than simply information on the latest in website technology.

The end result, we feel, is a jargon-free, readable introduction to creating compelling, interesting and user-friendly websites.

In addition, numerous pointers to online resources ensure that those who want to learn about the more advanced aspects of Web design will have plenty with which to occupy themselves.

This Book in a Nutshell

Chapter 1 outlines the steps you should take before you start creating your website.

Chapter 2 provides a guide to the process of designing the look and feel of your website, and deciding on the graphics and content you will need (and, more importantly, where to put them).

The benefits the Web offers those planning to use it for business are canvassed in **Chapter 3**.

Chapter 4 contains an introduction to the concepts and terminology of graphics, and features step-by-step guides to creating custom graphics for your website.

For those who haven't either the patience or the desire to create their own Web graphics, **Chapter 5** highlights some sources of free graphics that you can download and use on your site, while the basics of HTML - the "language" of the Web - are discussed in **Chapter 6**, and in **Chapter 7** we provide several examples of websites you can copy and experiment with.

Chapter 8 caters for those who don't want to get their hands dirty, and examines a leading, point-and-click WYSIWYG ("What-You-See-Is-What-You-Get") Web authoring tool.

Chapter 9 explains the process involved in "publishing" your website; that is, uploading your files to a Web server so that other users can access them.

Chapter 10 highlights important issues that all website owners should be aware of, while **Chapter 11** provides some pointers on how to get free publicity for your website.

Finally, **Chapter 12** turns a critical eye on some high profile - and some not so high profile - websites and applies many of the principles espoused in this book, so readers can see how they work in the real world.

Chapter 1

Planning your Website

When creating a website, one of the first - and most important - questions to ask yourself is: "Why do I want a website?" To answer, you will need to consider several issues:

- **What am I trying to achieve with my website?**
- **Who do I want to attract to it?**
- **What benefits will the website offer these people (and me)?**

Other considerations may include:

- **Is the site intended to make profit or be a labour of love?**
  Not all "profitable" websites are geared for online sales. Business sites may be designed to contribute to the business in other ways, such as reducing communication costs, maintaining customer loyalty and servicing interstate and overseas markets. Similarly, non-profit websites may still benefit their owners. For instance, many bands waiting for their big break are creating websites so they can distribute samples of their music online, in the hope of creating sufficient enthusiasm about their work to attract music labels and producers.

- **How much time and effort am I prepared to spend maintaining and updating the site?**
  Many people are not prepared for the amount of time that maintaining even a modest website can demand. Their site soon transforms from a stimulating, creative outlet to a burden. The Web is littered with thousands of "abandoned" websites.

- **Will the website consist primarily of links to other sites, or will it feature original content?**
  If the latter, where will you get content? Will you write it yourself, purchase it or seek contributions from similarly minded people?

Once you have examined the reasons for your site, and the purposes it will fulfil, you will be in a better position to plan and create it.

Plan, Plan and then Plan Some More

When planning your website you will save a great deal of time if you have everything at hand and have a firm understanding of your goals for the site. Prepare an outline of the information your website will contain, a list of images or graphics you want to use and a list of related websites (if you plan to offer visitors directions to sites of interest). To avoid duplication and omissions it's a good idea to work to a written plan, such as the one below:

- **Step 1**

    Decide who you are trying to attract to your website. A site designed solely as a gallery of photos of your newborn child and created for the benefit of relatives will have a ready audience. A would-be author looking to generate interest in a self-published work might find it harder to attract visitors to his or her site.

- **Step 2**

    Ask yourself what these users are likely to be interested in.

- **Step 3**

    Research existing websites that offer similar information or services. Look beneath the surface and examine how they have structured their site. Look at how it is laid out, how content areas, services and other offerings are defined and grouped. Note the Web tools they use to make the site more intuitive, entertaining and interactive. Form your own opinion of which aspects of the site are successful and which aren't (in terms of presentation, content and so on).

- **Step 4**

    Decide on the size of your site. How big (in terms of the number of Web pages) do you expect it to be?

- **Step 5**

    Gather the content for your website - the information, sounds and images visitors will read, hear and see.

- **Step 6**
  Prepare a flowchart or rough outline of the structure of your site, indicating which pages are interlinked and how, and showing the major pathways your visitors can follow as they explore the site. Having an idea of how each area of your website relates to the others will help you when preparing content and creating hyperlinks connecting each Web page and area. It will also help you analyse whether your proposed signposts, such as navigation icons, headings and the like, will make sense to visitors and help them move quickly, easily and intuitively between the various areas of your website.

  Once you are satisfied with your site structure, ask friends and colleagues for feedback. You'll be surprised how useful their insights will be, as they will be looking at your proposed site through the eyes of your visitors (something that many website creators find hard to do).

- **Step 7**
  If your website will be larger than a few linked pages, or a joint effort with friends or colleagues, it is a good idea to devise a timeline, to help map out the design and creation process.

- **Step 8**
  Consider any requirements your site may have that are beyond your skills, e.g. specialised graphics or animations, custom programming (for example, a search feature or shopping cart), security issues (ifyou plan to accept online orders) and the like. How will you overcome these problems? Hire a consultant? Call upon the skills of friends? Enlist a freelance Web writer or designer? If you don't resolve these issues before you start you may lose your "momentum" when you reach a stage requiring specialist skills.

- **Step 9**
  Once you have a firm idea of the purpose of your website, as well as a flowchart and a timeline, you should be in a position to accurately estimate the costs involved in publishing it. These will include your time creating and maintaining the site, Web hosting charges and any expenses incurred in hiring third parties to perform tasks beyond your skills.

We discuss the initial steps - defining your audience, researching and planning your site, and gathering content - briefly below, and in more depth in later chapters.

Design for your Audience

There are now millions of websites on the Internet, all competing for users' attention. Your goal should be to make your site stand out from the crowd. This can be the most challenging aspect of creating a website. The design, layout and content of your site should be carefully crafted to project the "image" you want and to grab the attention and interest of your target audience. A website promoting the services of a magician for children's parties may be fun, wacky or weird, while a website offering relationship-counselling services needs to project professionalism, trust and sincerity.

Above all - and you'll read this more than once in the following chapters - your site needs to "communicate" with your visitors. If your website doesn't communicate to readers in terms they can understand, all your efforts will have been wasted.

Explore other Websites

If you are uncertain of the type of design you should use on your website, spend some time wandering around the Web. Keep a note of which sites catch your eye and look carefully at the sites you don't like. Pick out the central themes at play in both kinds of sites (such as layout, colour and image usage, the ratio of text to graphics and so on), and decide what "works".

Pay particular attention to why you linger at a particular site, or why you want to leave it. Do the navigational tools (such as buttons and links) encourage you to explore the website, or do they hinder your progress through the site? Is the site easy to read, or is it cluttered or too brightly coloured? Does it load quickly, or must you wait for minutes at a time? What hooks and "teasers" does the site use to convince you to stay and explore for a little while longer?

Although it can be helpful to use other sites as inspiration for your own, be careful that your site doesn't become simply a collection of ideas from other sites. While this will probably save you time in the design process, it might result in your site losing identity. More importantly, it could result in a website that looks poorly planned.

Also, while it's a good idea to survey a broad range of websites to get a feel for what works online and what doesn't, be careful when it comes to borrowing ideas from sites that are designed with different goals to yours. What works on a website designed to promote magicians may not work for marriage counsellors.

Gather your Content

Once you have decided what you want your website to say, determined its audience, and considered its appearance, you will need to gather your content.

Before doing so, write a list of possible topics and points of interest. Ask friends or colleagues to read through the list and suggest which of your points are solid, interesting ideas and which are less important. Be prepared to act on the feedback you receive, eliminating points that are unnecessary or uninteresting.

Once you have outlined the content required for your website, ensure that it fits within your original plan for the site. You may need to review your overall purpose in light of the ideas you came up with, or vice versa.

Timelines

It is unnecessary to create a timeline if your site is purely for your amusement. However, a timeline will prove useful if others will be providing input or playing a role in the site's development. Your timeline should outline the total project time (be realistic!) and stipulate when each step of the project should be completed. It should also indicate when and how often the site will be updated.

Even if you don't manage to stick to the time constraints of your time-line, its development will help you order the processes involved in creating your site. Do you develop the content first and then create the pages needed to display it, or do you create the pages first and then write the content to fit? The answers to such questions will depend on the type of website you are creating and its purpose.

Special Requirements

Many websites will have special requirements. For example, if your site is quite extensive, and contains a large amount of content, you may wish to offer your users a search function so they can quickly locate information of interest. Similarly, if your website will be used as an online shopfront, you may incorporate some electronic commerce features, such as credit card verification and security.

Such issues are beyond the scope of this introductory text. However, there are many online sources of information that you can refer to for guidance.

If you choose to use consultants to provide programming or other services, it is still important that you determine both the nature of the special services you need and how these should behave, as this will form the basis of contracting with the consultants.

Costing the Project

There are a number of costs associated with publishing a website. Some of the more obvious include renting space on a server to host your site, and online charges incurred when uploading and testing the site. Other costs include special Web authoring and image-creation software, consulting and design services and the time invested by you or your staff in preparing and maintaining the site.

Be realistic when costing your project, so you know how much time and money to set aside for it.

Chapter 2

Designing your Website

Once you have planned your site, you should be ready to start work! A fun, intelligent, creative and clearly designed website will stand out from the crowd. While many websites might already offer the same information or services as your planned site, few will score highly in terms of both interesting content and appealing presentation.

The Essence of a Good Website

An effective design will present information in a clear, easy-to-read format, and make navigation straightforward and intuitive. It will allow visitors to quickly gauge what your website offers, and give them swift access to content that interests them. This holds true regardless of whether your website is a major corporate marketing initiative with a million dollar budget, or a personal Web page designed as a meeting point for a small circle of friends. If a visitor has to stop to puzzle over what you mean or where they can go next, you run the risk of losing them completely as they give up and go to another site.

Writing Style

Writing for the Web isn't quite the same as preparing a report or other business documentation. While your visitors want to read accurate, hype-free information, they don't want to feel as if they are wading through an annual report or internal memo. By all means research your content, and make it as accurate and reliable as possible. Pay close attention to grammar and spelling, as mistakes look unprofessional and can be quite distracting.

Unless you plan to restrict access to your site to a specific group of individuals, you will be communicating with an audience from a wide variety of backgrounds. Your writing style should be breezy, even conversational. Try to remember your first attempt to read high-school chemistry or biology textbooks. While these books are authoritative sources of information, their presentation and writing style can quickly bore even the most inquisitive minds. Many websites are like this. Their creators got carried away with being authoritative and exhaustive, and forgot that the basic aim of a website is to communicate. And while high school science students are (usually) motivated to try to make sense of their textbooks, Web users are not so forgiving.

Finally, study after study has shown that few people "read" websites - rather, they browse. Visitors want short, punchy sentences that quickly communicate facts and information. Use bullet points where necessary, and include headings and sub-headings so visitors can scan the text for specific information. The bottom line is that visitors won't plough through page after page of text to extract relevant information. Instead, you need to give it to them in bite-sized, readily identifiable and easily accessible portions.

Page Layout and Visual Design

Your site must include eye-catching graphics or headlines that immediately tell visitors what it offers. Visitors will leave rather than browse through several screens to discover the purpose of your website. Try to keep each page small enough to fit entirely within the user's screen. Many users won't scroll down to read information or look for options that they can't see right away. If you must have Web pages that are longer than a single screen, ensure all the important headlines and links are visible within the first screen.

Unfortunately, this advice is easier to give than it is to follow. As discussed in Chapter 4, the type of computer a visitor uses to access your site will affect its appearance, as will the type of monitor. For instance, a web page that fits comfortably in a single screen when viewed with a 15-inch monitor with a display area of 1024 x 768 pixels might scroll for two or more screens when viewed with a 14-inch monitor with a display area of 640 x 480 pixels.

The best solution therefore is to design for "the lowest common denominator". Until recently, this was a 14-inch monitor with a screen display area of 640 x 480 pixels. While many websites still use these dimensions, others now assume a minimum display area of 800 x 600 pixels. Given the affordability of new computers and monitors, it is probably safe to design your site for the larger screen. At the very least, you should test your website by viewing it with several different sized monitors.

Simplicity is Best

Be careful not to overcrowd your Web pages. Simplicity coupled with a little imagination is always more effective than a cluttered page. Maintain a sensible balance between content and illustrations. Unless the topic dictates an all-text or all-graphics website, break up long sections of text with subheadings, bulleted lists, and graphics. A screen full of text is very tiring to read.

Using Graphics

Graphical icons, horizontal dividers and other images can be used to present text on screen and to divide sections of information into logical or "bite-sized" portions. In addition, use graphics or clip art to demonstrate your points and to highlight sections of information.

Choose foreground and background colours that complement the graphics used. You should also ensure there is sufficient contrast between your background and foreground colours, as well as between your text and images so users don't need to strain to read your content.

Navigation

A crucial, but often underrated, aspect of a website is its navigational elements. Unless you are planning only a single-page site, you will need to provide visitors with a means of navigating through your website. Visitors can easily become disorientated in a badly structured site. If this happens, they may well decide that trying to find their way around is not worth the trouble.

Most websites revolve around a primary "home page". This is the opening page of a website that greets new arrivals and where visitors begin their exploration. Your home page acts as an introduction and gateway to the contents of your site, just as a magazine's cover introduces readers to its content.

Home pages generally lead with a catchy headline, banner or logo and a short introduction to the site, which tells visitors what the site offers and how it will benefit them. This is generally followed by a series of clickable hyperlinks that will take visitors to different sections of the site.

Traditionally, we tend to view information as a linear resource. For instance, when reading a book you generally start at the beginning

Communication

Research on Web browsing habits reveals that, as a general rule, a Web site needs to clearly communicate to the visitor why it is worth visiting within 10 seconds of their arrival, or they will be off to another Web site. Most Web users have short attention spans, because they pay for the time they spend online (which means their online time is limited) and there are a large number of interesting sites to visit.

Therefore, the guiding principle of Web design is: 'Design for the sake of communication, not simply for the sake of design.'

and read to the end. The Web and its power to hyperlink is transforming the way we use and absorb information, as it allows readers to choose the order in which they want to access information. Therefore, it's imperative to consider the site's navigational "pathways" as an integral part of the site's design.

The simplest form of navig-ation is to include a text-based overview of your site - such as a one- or two-paragraph description - on the home page, with links to various areas of your site. However, if your website contains many areas and corresponding pages of text, visitors might not wish to read through a lengthy site description to find areas of interest.

In such cases you might design your home page to act like a table of contents, providing a skeletal overview of - and links to - the major areas of your site. Each area might be represented on the home page by a topic summary featuring hyperlinked key terms or graphical icons that visitors can use to jump directly to that resource. To make their sites more appealing and intuitive, many designers use icons to represent different areas. Common examples are question mark icons ("?") to represent a link to the help (or "FAQ" -"frequently asked questions") section, and dollar signs ("$"), credit card symbols or shopping-cart icons to represent a link to the online ordering section.

If your website consists of more than a handful of pages, divide its content into logical sections, with a summary of each section on your home page. For example, imagine you are developing an online bookstore. How can you best categorise your content to create a neat, easy-to-follow navigational structure?

 **Start** Spot

 **Book** Spot

What you need before you read.

Click here to find: Book Reviews ▼

 **Library** Spot ™

Library Site of the
Reference Site of the
Sign up for our free
Add a library to your
——————————Friday,

Libraries
Libraries Online
Gov't Libraries
Image Libraries
Law Libraries
Medical Libraries
Music Libraries
Pres. Libraries
Librarian's Shelf

Reference Desk
Acronyms
Almanacs
Associations
Ask an Expert
Biographies
Business Info
Calculators
Calendars
Country Info
Current Events
Dictionaries
Encyclopedias
Genealogy
Government Info
How To
Maps
People
Quotations
Statistics
Style Guides
Tech Reference ᴺᴱᵂ
Thesauri
Time
White Pages
Yellow Pages
Zip Codes

Reading Room
Books
Journals
Literary Criticism
Newspapers
Newswires
Magazines
Poetry

Must-See Sites
Infoplease
Library of Congress
RefDesk.com
Britannica

Lists
Top 100 Comedies
Spelling Bee Winners
2000 Pulitzer Winners
Nat'l Bk. Critics Winners
Top 100 Languages
Best Books of '99
Best Newspapers
Top 100 Foundations
Top 50 Search Words
Top 100 Library Books
College Rankings
Top 10 News Stories
See more Lists...

Feature Archive
Medical Information
Continuing Education
Educational Resources
Favorite Books
Test Preparation
Literary Criticism
Virtual Field Trips
How To...
Homework Help
Getting Grants
Science Projects
Lesson Plans
Breaking News
Schools Online
Map It Out
Researching Companies

Genealogy Help

Start tracking your
roots online.

World's L
Libraries

Tour some o
largest collec

You Asked for It

- Where can I translate phrases/sites? ᴺᴱᵂ
- What's happening in the sky tonight?
- How do I raise a reader?
- Where can I search full-text articles?
- How much did that house sell for?
- How do I remove my name from lists?
- Where can I learn about movies?
- Who spoke at commencement?
- Can I search obituaries online?
- Where can I scan all the headlines?
- What happened on a particular day?
- How do I cite Internet sources?
- Find answers to more questions.

Do You Know

- How many newspapers are sold daily?

*The Library Spot arrange their links to offer an easy to navigate,
fun-to-use site... check out www.libraryspot.com*

You might decide to go for absolute simplicity, and offer only two options on the first page: fiction and nonfiction. If you have a reasonably small range of books this might work, and you could offer further navigation options on following pages. However, if your range is quite substantial, you will need a larger number of links on the first page to make the website more manageable. But before creating dozens of links, note that research has shown that the average person can only cope with a maximum of five choices at a time. Try to keep the number of menu options or navigation pathways on each page to five or fewer.

You may therefore decide to use the following categories: reference, sport, sci-fi, and best sellers. You also plan to rely heavily on reader reviews (supplied by customers), so you include a link to your book review section, taking the number of links on the first page to five. Obviously an online bookstore also needs more specific categorisation than that suggested above, so you decide to insert a second level of subcategory pages, each with no more than four subcategories. In essence, your overall site navigation plan will look similar to the flowchart shown below.

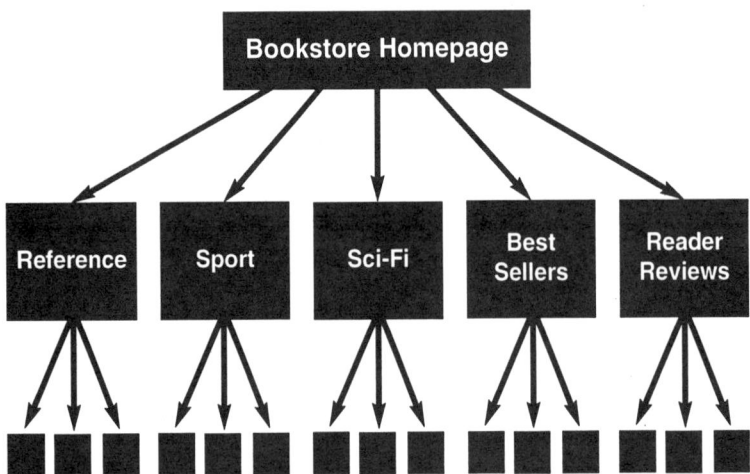

Avoid constructing overly complex sites. As a rule of thumb, users shouldn't have to click on more than three links within your site to find the information they want. Don't bury your content deep inside. Visitors may have a short attention span, and if getting to the content that interests them takes too long, they won't stick around!

One final point in terms of designing the flow of your website: there should be no "dead ends". Each page must allow visitors to access another page and should contain navigational items, even if they are simply "back to home page" or "return to previous page" links. Don't rely on your visitors being proficient with the use of the "Back" button or their browser's history list function.

Consistency

While the layout of your website is quite subjective, it is important that each page of your site conform to a certain "look" or template. Applying several different layout styles to the individual areas of your website might make it artistically impressive, but this will only confuse visitors, and rob your website of intuitive navigational cues. Imagine wandering around a supermarket with aisles more like a maze than the straight and narrow layout you're used to. Few would venture in, and those who did would probably give up before they got too far (or before they bought anything). Many website owners, in their attempt to create all-encompassing websites, unwittingly end up with confusing mazes, complete with ambiguous navigation cues and dead-ends - and visitors rarely stick around.

Predictable use of navigation icons, subheading styles and graphics will allow your visitors to clearly see the structure of your site. For example, consistently use a particular font size for the title of each new topic you introduce. Similarly, arrange any navigational icons in the same order, and display them in the same place on each page. If you use an icon to take visitors back to the home page, use the same icon on all pages to mean "go back to the home page" - and only use it for that purpose.

Avoiding Common Pitfalls

It can be easy to make mistakes the first time you design a site. Although the appearance and performance of your site will improve with practice, try to avoid the following common errors even in your early attempts.

Keep it Simple

One of the biggest mistakes users make when creating their first Web page is to include as many bells and whistles as possible. It's tempting to incorporate all the cool tricks you've seen at your fav-

Thumbnail Images

If you plan to use a number of large image files, as in the case of an online catalogue, consider creating 'thumbnail' images. This involves making a copy of the original image and saving it at a lower resolution and with smaller dimensions. The end result is a smaller image (in terms of both area and file size) that provides visitors with a preview of the original image.

For instance, a merchant selling paintings could display a thumbnail preview of each painting together with a text description. The thumbnails would download and be displayed on the visitor's screen quite quickly, and the visitor could then choose which to view full size.

ourite websites into your own - like flashing text, background music, animated icons, huge spinning three-dimensional logos and headings, scrolling text…the works. One of the first things that experience teaches you is: don't go overboard. Avoid run-of-the-mill website decorations, such as hit counters (do your visitors really care how many other people have seen the site?), repetitive scrolling announce-ments, and "under construction" signs (it's accepted that Web pages are under perpetual refinement). No one will be impressed with your "artistic talents" if your site is so overloaded with gimmicks that it is impossible to use, or takes ages to download.

Your site can be clever, imaginative and fun, but above all it should accomplish the purpose you decided on during the planning process. If you aim to showcase your skills as a designer, impressive tricks and graphics are certainly legitimate. But if your design efforts detract from communicating your message, you've failed.

Beware Proprietary Designs

The wide selection of graphics and other design tools available give Web designers the freedom to express themselves. While these tools can certainly simplify the creation of graphics and other multi-media, a few words of caution are in order. Web browsers have limited support for graphic formats. In fact, you can only safely assume that users will be able to view JPEG and GIF images (we discuss these formats in Chapter 4). Beyond that, compatibility issues may arise -

Hint

To learn more about Shockwave and see some examples of what can be done with the software, visit **www.shockwave.com**

If you don't already have the software required to view Shockwave animations, you will be prompted to download it when you visit the site.

not all browsers will be able to display your graphics.

The standard solution for compatibility problems is to provide "plug-ins" (programs that enhance the capabilities of Web browsers) designed to allow a browser to display or use specially created graphic and multimedia files. For example, Shockwave allows designers to add animation, cartoons and interactive games to websites. However, not all Web browsers support Shockwave file formats, so users must download and then install the Shockwave plug-in from www.macromedia.com/shockwave before they can view these files.

Many users will object to having to spend time downloading special software for the sole purpose of watching your new, whiz-bang introductory screen. In fact, most won't bother. Of those that do, some will experience problems installing the plug-ins (they can be difficult to install and configure), meaning they won't be able to view your site even if they want to. The best advice is to avoid using special file formats altogether. Alternatively, create two separate versions of your site - a "vanilla" version that uses standard text and graphics, and a "high-end" version that uses all the tricks you can lay your hands on - so your visitors have a choice. It is a different issue altogether, of course, if the purpose of your website mandates the use of the special software. For instance, many websites offering online training courses use multimedia programs, such as Shockwave and QuickTime (www.apple.com/quicktime), as the basis of their teaching methods. Other websites, such as news and cinema sites, offer online video clips. In such cases users would expect to download any software needed to make the most of the site.

Keep Performance Issues in Mind

It's important to remember that not everyone has the latest in PC technology. In fact, a large number of users still access the Internet using 486-based (and even 386-based) PCs, as well as older-style

Macs, such as the Mac Classic. Clusters of users even surf the Web with their much-cherished Amstrads, Commodores and Amigas! Take this diversity of PC hardware into consideration when designing your website. Although graphics might load quickly on your newer-model PC, they will be a little tardier on slower machines. Similarly, don't assume all viewers have special hardware. For instance, many Web users (especially those who access the Internet from work) don't have soundcards installed, preventing them from playing audio or music files. For this reason it would be foolish to design a site in which all navigational prompts are audible.

If an area of your website takes an especially long time to download, advise visitors of this. For example, if your site hosts an online sales catalogue with several high-resolution colour images on each page, advise visitors they can expect to wait for a certain amount of time (say, 30 seconds) for each of the images to down-load. This will reassure visitors that their browser hasn't crashed or that your site isn't malfun-ctioning. It also gives them the option of choosing to wait for the images to download, or moving on to another area of the site.

Some websites offer visitors even more choice. For inst-ance, a catalogue retailer might use fast-loading, low-resolution images on its main catalogue pages, but offer visitors the option of viewing high-resolution images if they want a closer look.

Browsers

One of the more annoying aspects of designing websites is that different Web browsers have different ways of doing things. While they all maintain a certain level of compatibility, each tries to outdo the others by adding their own special functions.

While taking advantage of these special functions might make developing your website easier, or allow you to add useful features, it is strongly recommended you maintain browser neutrality. Do not design your website with one Web browser in mind. Most Web authoring pack-ages can test your Web pages to ensure they will be viewed correctly by all Web browsers. Be sure to take advantage of this feature.

Keep the Object of the Game in Mind

Before adding bells and whistles to your site, ask yourself the following questions:

- **Does the feature enhance communication with my visitors?**

- **Will the feature be compatible with all Web browsers?**

- **Must users download special software for the feature to work? If so, will downloading present any difficulties?**

Aim to cater for the largest number of users. Not everyone:

- **Can view graphics when browsing the Web.**
  For example, some university students - who account for a large portion of the Internet user base - obtain Web access using network terminals that can only display monochrome text. In addition, many Web users configure their browsers not to display graphics, in order to speed up website access. For this reason, make sure you provide a text-only alternative, or at least provide text-based navigational elements;

- **Has a high-speed computer.**
  Therefore, some people may have difficulties viewing large animation files;

- **Has a high-speed modem.**
  Users may become impatient waiting for files to download;

- **Can (or wants to) listen to music while they browse;**

- **Will have all the plug-ins and other special software needed to take advantage of the latest multimedia trick;** or

- **Will have the latest version Web browser.**

Keep it Fresh
To encourage visitors to return to your website time and again you'll need to update it regularly. The frequency with which you need to update your content will depend on the nature of your site. For example, if your site is dedicated to following the progress of a famous golfer or football team, you should update it at least once a week - more often if games are played more frequently.

Hint

For more information about the efforts of Web designers worldwide to convince browser developers to develop agreed standards, see **www.webstandards.org**
   To find out more about making your Web site compatible with a broad range of browsers, see **www.anybrowser.com**

On the other hand, if your website is designed to keep track of the latest findings of a NASA probe, you need only update it whenever there is a new report of an interesting finding.

At the other end of the spectrum, if you operate a stockbroking firm and use your site to keep clients informed of the stock exchange's performance, you should update it at least hourly.

Resources

Sun Guide to Web Style   www.sun.com/styleguide
Web Developers Virtual Library   wdvl.internet.com
Yale Web Style Guide   info.med.yale.edu/caim/manual
Web Page Design for Designers www.wpdfd.com
Design-o-rama   www.glassdog.com/design-o-rama

Chapter 3

The Special Needs
of Business

Imagine for a moment that you own a clothes store in a busy shopping mall in an inner-city suburb. In the last few years, your store has endured flat consumer spending and pressures on profit margins. Although you've established market share, your cash flow is often barely enough to cover operating expenses such as inventory, rent, staff and advertising. In short, times are tough.

Now imagine that a stranger walks in and claims you can halve your advertising costs, reduce rent by more than two-thirds, slash operating stock expenses and never pay staff again. You'd think this was impossible. But this is exactly what many people say the World Wide Web can do - and it has plenty of vendors very excited!

An Automated Sales Medium

The Web has many uses, several of which we will examine in this chapter. However, the most widely perceived use for the Web is as an automated sales medium. The basic concept is simple, as it borrows many elements from the mail-order business model popular in the late eighties and early nineties.

In essence, a vendor establishes a website that contains an online catalogue of their products.

For example, the catalogue of a clothes shop would contain colour photos of each item of clothing (perhaps multiple photos to demonstrate different colours or sizes), together with a text description of the item. Consumers would visit the site, view the catalogue and place orders for items using their credit card. Such online catalogues offer many advantages:

- The vendor can display items and accept orders 24 hours a day, seven days a week;

- Customers on the other side of the globe find it as easy as local customers to view an online catalogue and place orders;

- The sales process - display, order placement and processing - is automated, reducing staff and associated overheads;

- There are no costly long-term leases and overheads as hiring space on a Web server is very inexpensive;

- The payment process can be automated, with funds automatically credited to the vendor's bank account;

- Paperwork - such as order forms, invoices and so on - can be minimised or avoided; and

- Inventories can be stocked on a "just-in-time" basis, freeing up capital.

Many businesses have incorporated the Web into their sales strategy - ranging from giants such as Argos at www.argos.co.uk, to smaller businesses and home-based companies. But the Web offers businesses more benefits than simply online sales.

Customer Service Functions

Many businesses find their website to be extremely profitable - though not only in terms of sales. Websites are ideally suited to customer-loyalty initiatives, helping businesses generate additional revenue from repeat sales while reducing overheads by automating customer-service functions.

Perhaps the best example of this sort of customer service is provided by the banking industry. Not long ago "doing the banking" meant a tedious routine of filling out a mountain of paperwork, driving to the branch, and then queuing for a teller. Today customers can make payments, arrange funds transfers, query account issues, and obtain balances and details of recent transactions - all without leaving their desks. The most impressive aspect of this type of online customer service is that all parties benefit.

Customers save time and reduce paperwork by accessing their account details and performing banking online. With the right software, customers can even "synchronise" their personal or company accounts and bank balances.

For instance, rather than have a bookkeeper manually reconcile business accounts, many businesses simply instruct their accounting software to query their bank's database and transaction records to verify the week's banking - a few hours' work accomplished in a matter of seconds.

Banks benefit too. As consumers migrate to online banking services, banks can reduce spending on staffing, consolidate branches and reduce floor-space requirements. This leads to more efficient service delivery, which is often reflected in reduced bank fees and enhanced profits.

Technical Support Functions

In order to maintain market share, most retail, industrial and professional sectors are under increasing pressure to make their products and services stand out from the crowd. Many companies are achieving this by offering better after-sales support. For instance, imagine your new car's engine started making an odd noise, which you think might be related to a loose fan belt. You could either take it to the nearest service centre (which might be inconvenient, as you will be without your car for part of the day), or try to resolve the problem yourself. This could be a simple task - if you're familiar with cars. But what if you're not? You could consult the owner's guide for pointers, or you could go out and buy a "fix-it" guide. Alternatively, you could call the manufacturer's maintenance help line (if they have one).

A faster, cheaper option would be to visit the website the manufacturer has created specifically for owners of its cars and read the information available on car maintenance. An online vehicle-maintenance site serves a number of purposes. Firstly, it provides vehicle owners with a valuable service that allows them to seek information about their car whenever they need it, regardless of the time of day. Secondly, from the manufacturer's perspective, it is a cost-effective means of providing extra value to clients, thereby making their vehicles more attractive.

More importantly, it allows the company to reduce customer-support overheads by decreasing the pressure on the maintenance help line - which translates to lower staff and telephone costs.

Marketing

Each year, businesses spend billions of pounds marketing products and services to consumers. We see commercials on TV, on videos and billboards, in newspapers and magazines, at the cinema and on the sides of cars and buses. We hear commercials on the radio, while on hold on the telephone, and as we walk around shopping centres. Some of this marketing is pretty much hit and miss (such as TV and radio advertising), while other campaigns are more focused (such as direct-mail catalogues).

The Web offers businesses a new marketing medium which allows vendors to target potential customers very specifically, either by setting up their own sites or by buying advertising space on other sites. If a pharmacy established a website, for instance, it could be confident that each visitor would constitute a "pre-qualified" consumer. In other words, with hundreds of thousands of other possible Web destinations, it's unlikely consumers would visit the pharmacy's website unless they were interested in the products or services on offer.

The site owner can therefore base the content and sales focus on the needs of the consumer and get straight down to the selling and educating process.

At the other end of the marketing spectrum, a golf-club vendor might choose to place banner ads promoting their products on a general sports website, or on a site related to golf (like the PGA's website, at www.pga.com). The vendor can be confident that visitors to sites displaying its advertisements will be interested in its products, as they have pre-qualified themselves by visiting sports-related websites. It is this level of targeting that most excites online vendors and advertisers.

Interactivity

The ability to interact with consumers has long been the goal of the marketing industry. Even the best-crafted print advert or the most visually appealing television commercial can only go part of the way to marketing a product or service.

For example, a travel agency might take out a full-page newspaper advertisement advising readers of its discounted Christmas flights. Because of the expense involved in such advertising, the travel agency can only promote a selection of these flights.

This can severely limit the effectiveness of the advertisement. First of all, not every reader will be interested in travel information or discounted flights. Of those who are, not all will be interested in the options mentioned in the advertisement. Therefore, the advertisement needs to have at least a twofold objective: to let those readers who are interested in specific travel products know what the agency is offering, and to convince those interested in other options to contact the agency. If it doesn't achieve both these objectives, then the travel agent has not maximised the benefits of its advertising.

The interactive nature of the Web means online advertising doesn't suffer from these limitations. For instance, a travel agency's website could list all of its products. More importantly, rather than bombard each visitor with a host of travel packages, the site could tailor packages to each customer's requirements.

For instance, a consumer interested in arranging a holiday during the Christmas season might connect to the travel agency's website. Here she is offered a few generic travel options, including cruises, tropical resort flight/hotel packages and ski holiday packages.

Liking the idea of spending Christmas in the snow, she clicks on that link and is taken to the section of the site marketing ski holidays. After reviewing the available packages, she doesn't find one that appeals to her. If she's going to go skiing, she'd like to visit Aspen, Hollywood's favourite ski destination, but there's not a specific Aspen package listed. However, the travel agency has included a "do-it-yourself" holiday planning utility.

Using the answers to a few specific questions (including preferred airline, accommodation preferences and the like), the agency's website scans its database of flights and other travel options and tailors a holiday package for the consumer. Delighted with the service and excited at the thought of spending Christmas in the snow, she books the trip and pays online with her credit card. Had the agency not been able to offer personalised service, it might have lost a sale. No other advertising medium allows the vendor to get this "close" to consumers, and respond to their specific needs.

Special Considerations
When planning and designing a website, businesses need to carefully consider their target audience, as this will affect both the content and appearance of the site.

The questions below will help you determine the nature of your target audience:

- **Geographic -**
  Does your site target users from a specific country, region, or city, or is its reach global? Are you likely to attract only English-speaking visitors, or will your site be multilingual?

- **Demographic -**
  What age group are you trying to attract? Is your potential visitor male or female, or is there no gender bias?

- **Psychographic -**
  What stage of life are your visitors in? Are they studying? Are they married with children? Are they working people?

- **Behavioural -**
  What personality traits are your audience likely to exhibit? For example, are they likely to be reserved and cautious or outgoing risk takers? What types of products and services are they likely to be interested in?

Having defined your target audience, your next step is to ensure that the design, layout and content of your website are attractive and stimulating to that audience.

If you wanted to attract adolescents to your website, for instance, you might draw heavily on popular techno-culture to create the impression that the site has some "street cred" and that it understands them. The cooler your site, the more likely those visitors will tell their friends (word-of-mouth advertising is the best way of attracting interested users to your website).

A good example of this type of presentation is the Seventeen Online website (www.seventeen.com). Its owners have created an effective - and cool - site using a kaleidoscope of bright colours, quick-read headlines and photos to get the reader's attention.

The MTV website (www.mtv.com) is aimed at a slightly older audience and uses a subtler, more sophisticated presentation and layout. That the colours, photos and layout mimics the style used on many music CD covers is not a coincidence - the site seeks to attract Web users interested in music and pop culture.

The Seventeen Online Web site (www.seventeen.com)
looks just right to target a teenage audience.

Websites aimed at a younger audience, such as children browsing with their parents, need a completely different look. These should appeal to the children by using bright colours, simple navigational options, interesting icons and other visual stimulation - while maintaining a "wholesome" appearance to convince parents they are appropriate places for children to explore. This kind of design can be found at Disney (www.disney.com) and SeussVille (www.randomhouse.com/seussville).

Websites aimed at business people need a completely different approach. Many corporate websites adopt conservative yet appealing colours, projecting an image of respectability and dependability. Text layout and images tend to mimic the designs used in business magazines - heavy use of blue and green (colours often associated with tradition and respectability) and subtle images that neither overpower the reader nor detract from the text.

A site of this type is FT(www.FT.com), the investment bible for financial whizzkids. It makes strong use of various shades of pink

KidsCom - instantly recogniseable as a child-friendly site.

- instantly identifying itself as the paper of the financial whizz, with white backgrounds, giving a crisp, efficient and familiar look.

It's a good idea to take a look at sites that fulfil a similar role to that of your planned site. For instance, if you are considering creating a website to sell gift baskets featuring homemade jam to higher-income online shoppers, examine sites offering similar gift items. If you plan to sell to teachers, take a look at educational sites. Even if you plan to hire a Web design consultant to create your website, it's

Hint

Remember that everyone who visits your Web site is a consumer, even if they don't actually purchase goods from it. They consume information as well as products and providing useful, interesting information will encourage visitors to return (and perhaps make a purchase) and will build goodwill.

still important that you have a clear vision of how the finished product will look. If you have the design aspects of your site worked out to your own satisfaction (even if you don't plan the fine details of each page), you will be able to better brief your consultant, and save yourself time and money.

Resources

There is probably more "Web print" devoted to the business potential of the Internet than any other topic. The resources below will prove invaluable to anyone who wants to learn more about the best ways of using the Internet for business:

InternetWorld	www.internetworld.com
eRetail.Net	www.eretail.net
Doing Business Online	www.canbus.com/dbo/cbnews.htm
EMarketer	www.e-land.com
Internet Week	www.internetwk.com
Marketing & E-commerce	www.wilsonweb.com
Electronic Commerce Guide	e-comm.internet.com

Chapter 4

Graphics for Beginners

It's hard to imagine, but when the Web was first launched, it was very much a text-only affair. In the early nineties, scientists and other academics primarily used the Web as a platform for distributing research data, scientific papers and journals. Most accessed it from computer terminals that could only display very simple text - images were useless.

Today, you can't wander anywhere on the Web without seeing images. They are used to identify websites and products, for decoration, and as an integral part of the site (such as the icons incorporated in navigational systems). Increasingly, news and information services are including photos and online video footage to illustrate events happening around us. This chapter shows you how to prepare your own images, including logos and banners. But first, it's useful to cover some technical terms and concepts.

Image Formats

There are two main image formats used on the Web: JPEG and GIF. These are currently the only graphic formats that all Web browsers, on both Windows and Macintosh, can display without the need for special software. The bulk of the images you will come across online will be either JPEG or GIF images (denoted, respectively, by the .jpg or .gif file extension).

JPEG (pronounced "jay-peg"), stands for Joint Photographic Expert Group, the name of the standards group that created the format. JPEG image files use data-compression techniques known as "lossy compression" to reduce the file size of stored images. Although some of the image data is lost in the compression process, the overall image quality is not affected adversely.

The JPEG image format is mainly used for digitised photographs and "continuous tone" images (images that contain large areas of the same colours), which tend to cope with the data loss inherent in the compression process. JPEG images are preferable to the GIF format for photograph-quality images because GIF graphics are limited to a 256-colour palette, whereas JPEG files can have a much larger number of colours. GIF, pronounced either "giff" or "jiff" (depending on whom you ask), stands for Graphics Interchange Format. All the data in a GIF image is preserved, with the result that GIFs tend to be larger than JPEGs. The GIF image format (also referred to as GIF89a, GIF87 or CompuServe GIF) is mainly used for indexed-colour (flat-colour) graphics. These images use fewer or less-complex colours.

Most image creation and editing programs support both of these formats (as well as many others) or allow you to convert image files into these formats. Many also offer an "export" function, which allows you to save an existing image file in a different graphic format. For example, you might load and modify a GIF image, then export it to the JPEG format. If your image-editing software doesn't offer an export function, you might be able to achieve the same result via the "Save As" option.

JPEG or GIF?

One of the key issues when preparing graphics for the Internet is file size - the smaller the better. (See Chapter 10 for a discussion of the issues raised by file sizes.) The smaller the size of the image file, the faster the visitor's Web browser can download and display it. Because of the different ways in which the two formats compress and store various types of images, it is not simply a matter of choosing one format and sticking to it. You will have to experiment until you get a feel for which file format is better (in terms of both file size and image quality) for the types of images you are creating.

Incidentally, when you save an image in JPEG format, most image creation software will allow you to specify the level of compression you want - in other words, how much you want the software to "squash" the file. Remember that the JPEG format uses "lossy compression", with the result that higher levels of compression lead to lower image quality. When creating JPEG images for your website, therefore, experiment with different compression levels to find the best balance between image quality and size. Save each image you create in both formats, playing with the colour palettes on GIF files and the compression levels on JPEG files. This might seem tedious at first, but you'll soon develop an understanding of the benefits and disadvantages of each format.

Hint

High-quality, interesting content is the most important aspect of your Web site. Everything else is secondary. Users will forgive a clumsy navigational system if you offer great content, but they won't forgive poor content, no matter how well it is presented.

Transparent and Interlaced Images

You might notice that your graphic-creation program gives you the option of saving GIF files as either transparent or interlaced images. Ordinarily, GIF images are stored in a "linear" fashion, which means they are downloaded and displayed line by line (from the top of the image downwards). With larger files it may take some time before the complete image appears, or to show enough detail to allow the user to ascertain what the image is.

An interlaced image is stored in a non-linear manner, so that a Web browser can depict a blurry façade of the entire image in one pass. As more image data is down-loaded, the image quality is sharpened, until the complete image is displayed.

Interlacing is handy when you can't avoid large images, but don't want users to become impatient while downloading. Interlacing allows users to choose between waiting for the entire image to download or seeing simply an outline before moving on. Interlaced images are also useful when an image appears at the top of the page with text underneath. Web browsers will download enough of the image to display an outline, then download and display the text before retrieving the rest of the image data. Visitors therefore don't have to wait for the full image to download before they can read the contents of the page.

A transparent image allows the background colour of a website to show through a GIF image whenever a specified colour - or no colour - is present in the image. For example, you might create a rectangular banner containing the word "Welcome" in red type on a blue background. Viewed alone, the image looks fine. But when you place that image on a Web page that has a white background (or some colour other than blue), its blue background appears as an unsightly coloured square on the white page.

The example Web page contains two versions of the same image (the word "welcome") — the image on the left is not transparent, while that on the right is.

Rather than create multiple banners with different background colours, you can save the image as a transparent GIF, with the blue background as the transparent area. The background of the transparent GIF will automatically match the background colour of the page, so the image integrates well. For instance, if you put an image containing the word "Welcome" in red type on a blue background on a Web page with a white background, the blue background will be displayed as a blue rectangle. If you put the same image with a blue transparent background onto a Web page with a yellow background, the blue section will be displayed as yellow.

Not all image creation programs will allow you to save images as transparent GIFs, but most of the popular programs will. For instance, Paint Shop Pro allows users to specify the transparent colour in an image. Colour transparency settings are generally only available when you are saving or exporting an image.

Image Resolution

"Resolution" describes the quality (in terms of sharpness and clarity) of an image. The higher the resolution, the better the image quality. Resolution is often measured in dots per inch of screen space (a dot is the smallest identifiable part of an image), or "dpi". The higher the dpi, the clearer and sharper the image.

The average computer monitor can't display images at a resolution higher than 72dpi. Compared to print resolutions (most books and magazine images are printed at 2400dpi) this seems quite poor. But 72dpi offers good display quality for most images.

Image creation programs will normally save images at a higher resolution (usually between 150dpi and 300dpi), unless you request that they be saved at a lower resolution. Given that higher resolutions mean larger files, and that high resolutions are wasted on most monitors, it doesn't make sense to save images at a higher resolution than 72dpi.

Image sizes

Image size is a vexing issue. On one hand, the larger the image, the easier it is to see, and the more information it can contain. On the other hand, larger images lead to larger file sizes. The average computer monitor is configured to display either 640 x 480 pixels or 800 x 600 pixels (more on these in a minute). Therefore, a 200 x 200 pixel image will occupy around one-sixth of a 640 x 480 monitor. This might be a good size for a corporate logo (which you'll want to display prominently), but it is too big for navigational icons which would soon fill up the screen area. And if viewers have set their browsers to display at smaller than full screen, the problem of crowding becomes even worse.

So, in addition to image resolution, you need to experiment with image size. Your images need to be legible (remember, not everyone has 20/20 eyesight), but they must not dominate the screen. For the technically minded: a pixel is actually comprised of three separate dots, but they are displayed so closely together that they appear connected. As mentioned earlier, most standard-sized monitors will display at least 640 x 480 pixels. So, a standard-sized monitor configured to the default setting has 480 vertical lines each containing 640 pixels displayed horizontally across the screen's viewable area - that should give you some idea of just how small pixels are!

Web-friendly Graphics to the Rescue

While most graphics programs allow users to create graphics optimised for the Web in terms of size and resolution, many require that the user be familiar with file formats and special menu functions. A new breed of graphics program targeting Web graphics is emerging, with programs such as Macromedia Fireworks (www.macromedia.com/software/fireworks). These programs promise to simplify the task of creating images for the Web, offering enhanced compression (to make files smaller), better colour support and extra features such as animation. Unfortunately, "professional" graphics programs generally come at a price, and these are no exception.

However, a number of cheaper programs now on the market have an "auto-optimise" function, which allows you to play with image size and quality settings before saving the file.

Step-by-step Banner Creation

Painting (Mac)
File size: 737K
Version: 1.6
Official website: www.sarwat.net/painting

Painting is an easy-to-use shareware ($US20 registration fee) paint program for the Mac. Unlike many other shareware programs, users are provided with documentation, including an 11-page "mini-manual" that will get most people working productively.

This is a neat little program for those new to the world of graphics. It doesn't have some of the features of the more upmarket professional graphics suites, but it has all you need to get started.

The Tool Palette
If you have ever used a "paint" or image-editing program before, you'll quickly become familiar with Painting's tool palette.

It provides single-click access to all the tools you need to create and edit your own graphics. Before jumping into creating a banner, take a look at Painting's main tool palette options.

When creating your own images, you must start with an appropriately shaped "canvas" (that is, the blank area that forms the basis of your graphic).

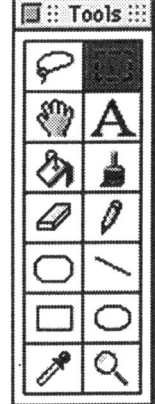

To mark out the canvas area, use either the Lasso or Rectangle tool. To create a rectangular canvas (used for banners or traditional logos), click on the Rectangle tool, then click your mouse within Painting's main window. Without releasing the mouse button, "drag" the mouse pointer until you have drawn a rectangle of suitable dimensions. When you release the mouse button, the screen will show the newly marked rectangular canvas. The Lasso tool works in the same manner, except that you can create "freehand" shapes.

Once you have created your canvas, you can move it, or images and text within it, using the Hand tool (represented by the hand icon). Click on the Hand tool, then click on the object you wish to move. The Text tool (represented by the "A" icon) is used to type text onto the canvas. Click on the Text tool, then place your mouse pointer at the position where you would like to insert the text. (The following tutorial discusses the Text tool in more detail.)

The Paint Bucket tool (this icon looks like a slightly tilted bucket) allows you to colour parts of your image. To do this, click once on the icon and then on the desired colour on the colour palette. Now click your mouse pointer on the area you want to "fill" with the new colour. To colour a smaller area, use the Paint Brush tool (represented by a brush-like icon). This works in the same way as the Paint Bucket tool: simply click on the icon, select your preferred colour from the colour palette, then click on the area of the image you wish to paint.

The Eraser tool "removes" parts of your image (for example, when you have wrongly painted in an area). To erase part of an image, click on the Eraser icon, and then click on the area that you wish to erase. You can erase larger areas by "dragging" the mouse pointer.

To add fine lines to your image, use the Pencil tool, which lets you draw lines one pixel thick. If you want to draw straight lines, depress the Shift key - and keep it depressed - while using the Pencil tool. To draw a rounded rectangle, an ellipse or a straight line, use the Rounded Rectangle, Ellipse and Line tools respectively.

Finally, to get a closer look at part of your image (for instance, when you are erasing or using the Pencil tool), click on the Zoom tool (which looks like a magnifying glass) and then on the area you wish to magnify.

The Colour Palette

Painting's colour palette contains the standard range of base colours (such as red, blue and green), as well as a variety of custom colours, such as cadmium yellow.

Fill and Stroke

Two terms you should acquaint yourself with when using Painting (or any paint program) are fill and stroke. Fill refers to the colour used for the "inside" of an object, while stroke refers to the colour of the outline. For example, when drawing a rectangle, you might make the fill (the main area) red, but the stroke (the outline) black. It is possible, of course, for the fill and stroke to be the same colour, but many users prefer to use a different stroke in order to give their images better contrast.

To specify the fill colour, click on the Fill icon (which has an image of a tipped bucket on it) and then on the desired colour from the palette. Similarly, to specify stroke colour, click on the Stroke icon (which shows a diagonal line) and then on the desired colour. Both icons are located in the top-left corner of the colour palette.

Creating a Banner for Your Web Page

Banners can be used for a number of purposes. The most common is a hyperlink advert placed on other websites to direct traffic to your site. For example, you might create a banner advertising ice cream and arrange to have it displayed on several recipe or food-related sites. Visitors to those sites may read your banner and, if they are interested, click on it. Their browser will immediately connect to your site. You can also create banners to use on your own website. For example, each page on your site might contain a banner advertisement for a product or service offered in a different area of the site. This helps to tell your visitors about what you have on offer.

In the following tutorial you will create a basic rectangular banner containing text on a coloured background.

Step 1: Create the Banner Shape
Select File from menu bar, click on New to create a blank canvas.

Step 2: Select a Colour
Select the background colour for your banner by clicking on a specific colour from the colour palette. Then, using the Rectangle tool, "drag" your mouse cursor to create a rectangular canvas of the size you want. Once you release the mouse button, the screen will show a rectangular canvas of the selected colour, shown overleaf.

Step 3: Insert the Text
To insert your banner text, click on the Text tool (the "A" icon on the tool palette) and then click on your banner canvas. A Text dialog

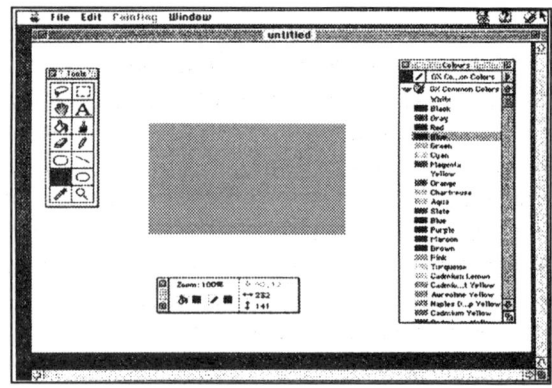

Use the Rectangle tool to resize your canvas.

box will appear. Within this dialog box you can enter the text which you want to appear in your banner, as well as modify the size, style (such as italics or bold) and font of the text, as shown below .

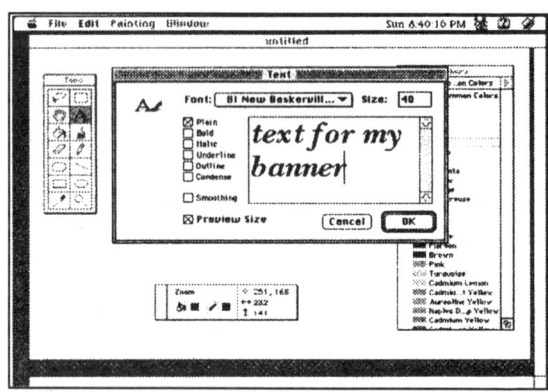

Use the Text tool to add text to your banner.

There are a wide range of fonts available, so spend some time experimenting with different fonts until you find one you like. Make sure that the font you choose is easy to read. Once you are happy with the appearance of your text, click on the OK button to close the Text dialog box.

Step 4: Position your text
Once you close the Text dialog box, your text will appear on the banner canvas, see below. While it is still highlighted, move it into position. To do this, click on the text and, while holding the mouse button down, drag it into position.

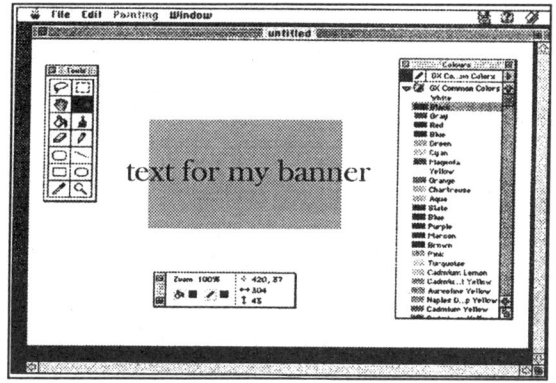

The next step is to align your text within your banner

—

you may need to resize the text so it will fit.

To edit the text, open the Text dialog box again by double-clicking on the text itself. Once you are satisfied with the text, size, style and positioning, click anywhere on the canvas (except text) to finalise the text insertion.

Step 5: Save your Banner
To save your banner, click on the File menu, then select Save. The Save dialog box will appear, as shown below. Painting will allow you to save your banner in JPEG format, so that you can use it immediately.

Last step — saving a copy of your creation.

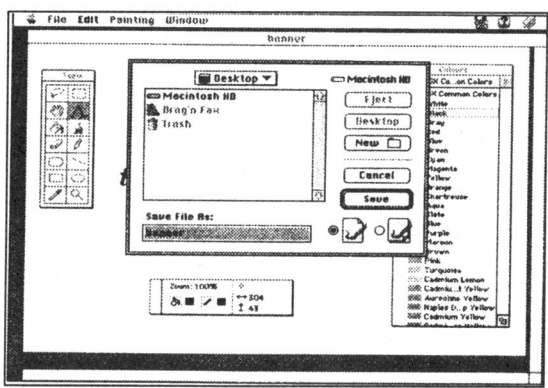

Be sure to experiment with the JPEG Image Quality option (available from the JPEG Options button, shown above right) so that you can see the correlation between image quality and file size.

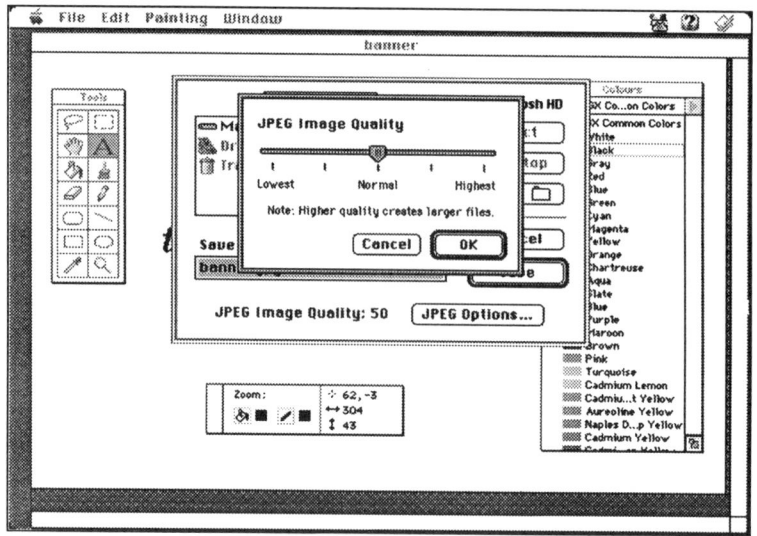

Experiment with the Image Quality options and find the best balance between file size and image quality.

Paint ShopPro (Windows)
File size: 14Mb
Version: v.6 (Windows 95/98/NT/2000)
Official website: www.jasc.com

Here we'll create a banner using the Windows shareware program Paint Shop Pro. Paint Shop Pro is a very popular program among both amateur and professional graphic artists.

Its popularity rests on both its low cost and excellent range of professional image-creation and editing tools. Paint Shop Pro can capture images from Web cameras directly to the image-editing canvas, and also includes an image-animation program - Animation Shop - that allows you to make animated buttons and images for the Web. Many of the tool-palette options available in Paint Shop Pro are the same as or similar to those discussed in the Painting tutorial. For further information about the toolbar options, take a look at Paint Shop Pro's extensive Help menu. Or try the handy collection of online tutorials at www.jasc.com/tutorials.html

Creating a Blank Canvas

To create a new, empty canvas, select New from the File menu or click on the New button on the toolbar. In both cases, the New Image dialog box will appear. From here you can specify various aspects of the canvas, including its dimensions, image resolution and colour. The settings shown in the New Image dialog box are suitable for a medium-sized banner, but you

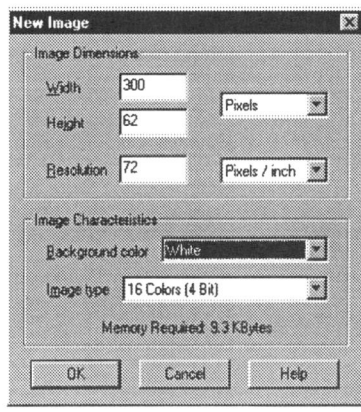

can experiment with the settings to determine the shape and dimensions most suited to your project.

Once you are happy with your settings, click on OK. Paint Shop Pro will then display your new canvas on screen. It should show the canvas actual size, so the finished product will be the same size as the on-screen image, allowing you to judge how it will look on your website, see below.

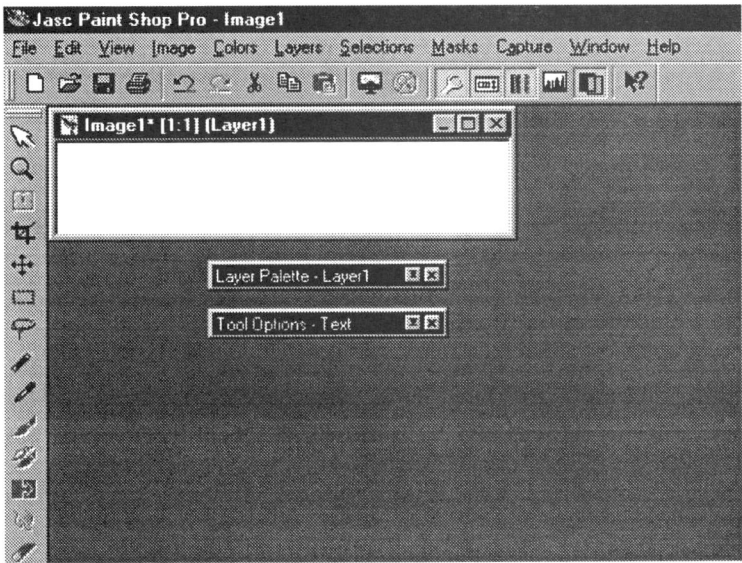

Paint Shop Pro's editing window looks complex, but you will soon get used to it.

If this image is too small to work with (in terms of adding and repositioning text), you can zoom in to magnify it. This doesn't alter the size of the image itself, but enlarges your view of it while you work. To magnify the image, click on the Zoom icon, represented by a magnifying glass in the Tool palette on the left-hand side of the Paint Shop Pro window, then click on the image itself. Each time you click the image, the level of magnification increases. To decrease the magnification (that is, to zoom out), click the right mouse button.

Colouring your Banner

On the right-hand side of the Paint Shop Pro window you will see a box displaying the full spectrum of available colours (known as the Colour Palette), beneath which are two squares with arrows pointing between them. The colours displayed in these squares represent Paint Shop Pro's default foreground and back-ground colours. The top square shows the current foreground colour, while the lower indicates the background colour.

There are two ways to change the foreground or background colours. The first is to move your mouse pointer over the desired colour in the Colour Palette. The mouse pointer changes to an eye dropper icon. To change the foreground colour, click your left mouse button on the desired colour. To change the background colour, click your right mouse button on the desired colour.

Alternatively, click your mouse pointer in either of the two squares. This will display the Select from Color Palette dialog box, allowing you to choose from a range of available colours. The number of available colours will depend on how many colours you chose in the New Image dialog box. (I chose to limit my colour palette to 16 colours in order to keep the resulting file as small as possible, so I only have 16 colours to select from.) Select your colour by clicking on it once to highlight it, then click OK.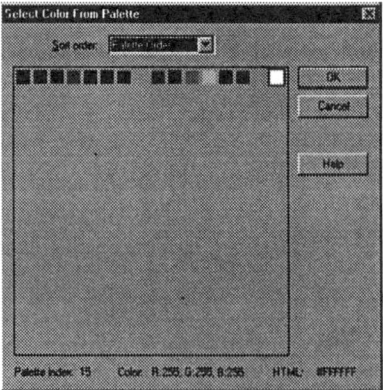

Once you have selected your foreground and back-ground colours, click on the Flood Fill tool in the Tool palette (represented by the "tipped bucket" icon) and position the mouse pointer over the canvas. To change the colour of the canvas to the foreground colour you selected, click once using the left mouse button. To use the selected back-ground colour, click the right mouse button.

If you change your mind about the background colour, it is best to change the colour before you begin inserting text.

Inserting Text

Text is inserted using the Text tool (depicted on the Tool palette with an icon in the form of a capital "A"). When your text is inserted, it will be the same colour as that specified as your foreground colour. If you want to use a different colour for your text, be sure to change your default foreground colour before using the Text tool. To insert your text, click on the Text tool icon and then click on the banner canvas in the general area you want your text placed. (Notice that the mouse pointer now appears as a kind of cross-hair icon with a capital "A".)

The Text Entry dialog box will appear, allow-ing you to enter your text and select the font you wish to use (including its style and size) as well as several other text attributes.

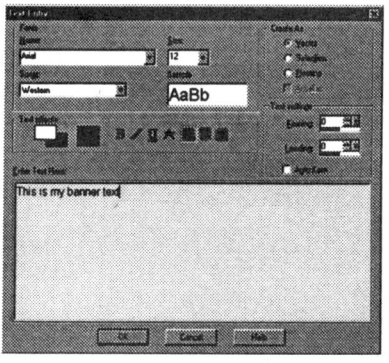

Paint Shop Pro provides a wide selection of fonts and styles. Your banner text will be displayed in the Text Entry dia-log box in the selec-ted font, so you can see what it will look like before making a final decision. Once you are satisfied with the appear-ance of the text, click the OK button to insert it into the canvas. The text will "float", allowing you to position it as you wish. The text is placed within a frame, which has small boxes located at key points (such as on each corner and in the centre). To move the text, click on one of these boxes and drag it while holding down the left mouse button.

To change the wording, font or appearance of your text at this stage, simply delete it (either using the Del key, or by selecting Cut from the Edit menu) and start afresh.

Once you are happy with the text, click on it with the right mouse button to finalise its insertion into your banner.

Saving your Image

To save your banner, select Save or Save As from the File menu, use the F12 function key shortcut or click on the Save toolbar icon, which looks like a floppy disk. The Save As dialog box will appear.

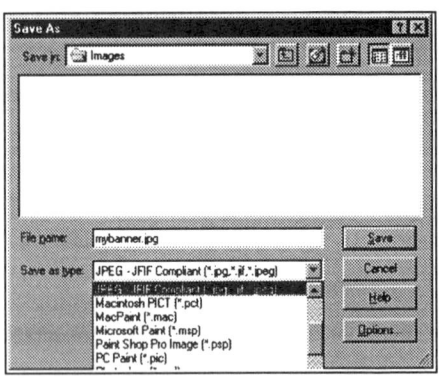

When you save your image, you will be given the opportunity of setting any available preferences. Specify a name for your banner, and then select your preferred graphic format - either JPEG or GIF - using the Save As Type drop-down menu. You can check the default graphic settings using the Options button.

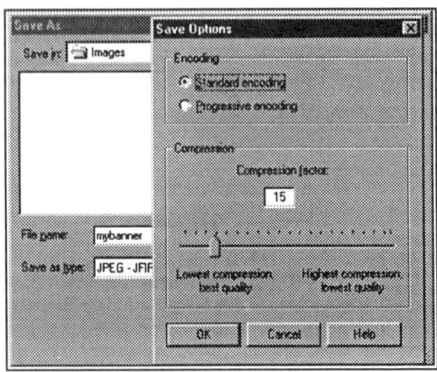

Finally, if you want to save your file in a directory other than that currently displayed, you can specify a new directory using the standard directory options. (The options available in the Save As dialog box are shown, right.) We discuss how to display your banner and, where applicable, make it behave as a hyperlink in Chapters 6 and 8.

Resources

Web Graphics on a Budget   www.mardiweb.com/web/

Creating Graphics for the Web www.widearea.co.uk/designer/

Bozine Web Graphics Help   www.bozine.com/helppages.html

Chapter 5

Free Images for your Website

Not everyone has the time, patience or inclination to create their own graphics. But this doesn't mean your website is destined to look plain and dreary. There are plenty of free images (including animated icons) and other graphics available on the Web.

When is Free Actually Free?

Before you get the wrong idea, this is probably a good time to explain the "etiquette" of image borrowing. The person who creates an image, whether it is a corporate logo or a simple little navigational icon, owns that image and retains the copyright to it. Therefore, as a general rule, it is not only wrong to "borrow" images from another website, but it may also be illegal.

If you see an image on a website that you absolutely must have, email the Webmaster or owner of the website and ask whether you can take a copy for your site. In most cases the creator will be flattered that you like the image and will give permission!

Image Warehouses

Although you should always be wary of borrowing images without permission, there are plenty of resources for free, public-domain images. Many websites are devoted to giving away copies of icons and other graphics. In such cases, there are no problems with downloading and using the images on your own website. You'll find hundreds of freebie sites online, and the following sites should get you started:

Fantasyland Graphics	www.enchantress.net/fantasy/index.shtml
Andy's Art Attack	www.andyart.com
Free Art	www.mcs.net/~wallach/freeart/buttons.html

Syruss' Graphics	www.syruss.com
Icon Bazaar	www.iconbazaar.com
Graphic Station	www.graphicstation.com
Site Builder Gallery	www.microsoft.com/gallery

Media Builder Graphics Library

www.mediabuilder.com/graphicsfree.html

The Free Site	www.thefreesite.com/freegraphics.htm
Xoom Free Clip Art	xoom.com/xoom/web_clip_empire

Free Banners

Banners are simply large rectangular graphics, which are reasonably simple to make (as shown in the previous chapter). However, as they are often used to promote a website or specific products and services, banners tend to be very specific in terms of looks and content. (We discuss banner advertising and other methods of promoting your website in Chapter 11.) As such, it's unlikely you will find any suitable banners in free Web collections.

But this doesn't mean you have to do without. A number of websites offer automated banner creation services: simply type in the words you want to appear in your banner, select from a range of different styles and - hey presto! - a new banner.

In the following example we will use the free Banner Generator service at www.coder.com/creations/banner. You'll find a list of other banner creation sites at the end of this chapter.

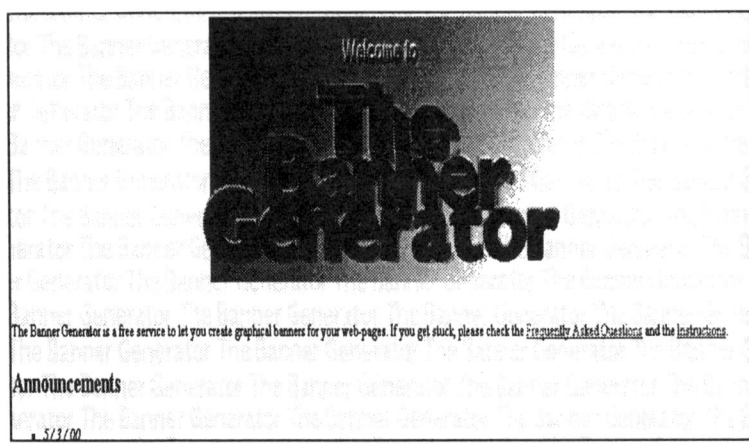

www.coder.com/creations/banner

Enter the text you want to appear on your banner, then select the font you wish to use.

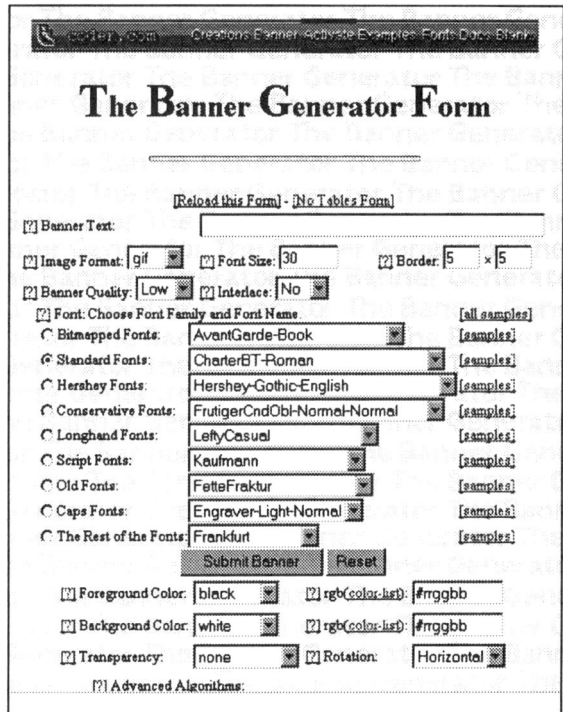

The first step is to complete the Banner Generator Form (see above), which you access via a link on the Banner Generator home page. Enter the text of your proposed banner, and select the graphic format you wish to create (GIF or JPEG) and the size you wish your banner to be. Each option has a help section, which can be accessed by clicking on the "?" symbol beside it.

Once you have specified the banner's contents, format and dimensions, you must decide on a font. There are a number to choose from and plenty of examples to help you make up your mind. Next, select the background and foreground colours you wish to use, and finally choose a special effect from those offered.

Once you have specified the parameters for the banner, click on the Submit Banner icon.

Within a few seconds you will be shown a screen confirming that your banner has been created, with information on how to view it. Your banner might look similar to the one shown overleaf.

Making banners is EASY!

Now save the banner to your hard disk, as discussed in the following section.

Saving Graphics

Downloading and saving copies of images for your own use is quite a simple task. If you see a graphic you want to download, click on it with your right mouse button and select Save Picture As from the drop-down menu that appears. Mac users can access the same menu by clicking on the image and holding the mouse button down.

The Save Picture dialog box will appear, allowing you to name the file and select the directory to which you want to save it. You can't, however, change its extension - it must remain .gif or .jpeg.

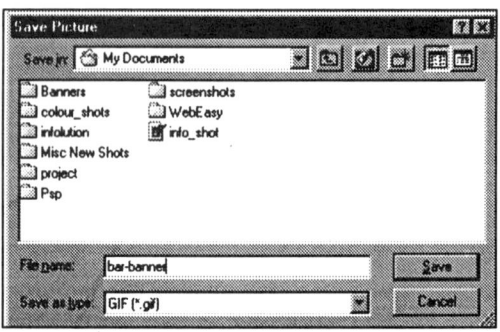

It's generally a good idea to store the images in the same directory as your other Web files - this makes them easier to manage and use.

Resources

Instant Online Banner Creator	www.crecon.com/banners.html
MediaBuilder Banner Maker	www.mediabuilder.com/abm.html
CoolText.com	www.cooltext.com
3D Logo Generator	wafu.netgate.net/3dlogo/e3dlogo.html
CoolBE	www.coolbe.com
Banner Tips	www.bannertips.com
QuickBanner	www.quickbanner.com

Chapter 6

Hypertext Markup Language (HTML)

This chapter is designed as an introduction to Hypertext Markup Language (HTML). Given the recent progress in developing truly what-you-see-is-what-you-get, point-and-click Web authoring packages, few new Web authors will ever need to learn the nitty-gritty of HTML. In fact, even the greenest Web author can now create professional-looking websites without writing a single line of HTML.

Even so, a broad understanding of HTML can be beneficial, especially if you want to take advantage of its more advanced features, such as tables.

User control

It's important to realise from the start that ultimately you don't control the look of your website. Instead, your visitors do, based on the preferences set in their browsers. For example, one visitor may prefer to use the Times New Roman font to display the content of your website, while another might use Helvetica - a very different look. Yet another user might set their browser to reduce loading time by not displaying any graphics. Some users keep the browser window small, while others choose to use the entire screen.

These preferences affect the appearance of your Web pages on the user's computer. Although HTML allows you to specify how you want your page to look, each user's preferences play a major role in how it actually appears. This aspect of Web design alone is reason enough to keep your website simple - a balance of graphics and well-spaced text is best.

HTML 101

The Hypertext Markup Language is essentially a collection of commands - called tags - that are integrated into text documents and interpreted by Web browsers. The tags themselves are English words or abbreviations, contained in angle-brackets (< and >).

Generally, tags are case-insensitive, so you can use either upper or lower case, although you need to keep in mind that most tags come in pairs and each tag of the pair must be in the same case. It is generally preferable to use upper-case for tags, as it makes them easier to find when you are editing HTML documents. Each pair of tags has a beginning tag and an end tag (the end tag is denoted by the use of the slash "/" character):

```
<TAG>
...
</TAG>
```

Most tags define what is to be done with the text between them. For example, text within the boldface tags (<B> and </B>) will be displayed in bold on the viewer's computer screen.

It is important to use tags in a structured manner. This becomes imperative when you are designing Web pages that will be viewed by visitors using different Web browsers. It will also be a great help when updating or revising documents. As you start creating more advanced Web documents it may be impossible to avoid nesting tags; that is, using tags within tags. However, as a general rule, nested tags should be avoided. While nesting is not as great a problem with the latest Web browsers, earlier versions of some browsers often interpreted nested tags in different ways (in some cases rendering Web pages unviewable). For instance, the following tags:

```
<TAG1>
...
<TAG2>
...
</TAG2>
</TAG1>
```

might be interpreted differently by different Web browsers, with the result that your Web page might be displayed incorrectly on the viewer's computer screen.

HTML documents that avoid unnecessary nesting will also be significantly easier to edit, revise and "troubleshoot".

Beware Non-Standard Tags

Before we take a look at the basic HTML tags, a word of warning. Although there are agreed "standards" regulating the way in which HTML tags are interpreted by Web browsers, the creators of various Web browser programs, especially Internet Explorer and Netscape Navigator/Communicator, have also developed their own, proprietary tags. Such non-standard HTML tags are only supported by a particular Web browser. Where possible, avoid using non-standard HTML tags. By using only those tags accepted as standard by all Web browsers, you can be assured your Web pages will be displayed properly on the viewer's computer screen, completely independent of the computer or Web browser they are using.

Document Tags

Document tags identify the beginning and end of a Web page and provide Web browsers with certain information about the Web page itself (for example, its title).

The <HTML> and </HTML> Tags

The first line of every Web page should consist of the <HTML> tag. This indicates to Web browsers that this is the beginning of the page. The corresponding HTML end tag is </HTML>, used at the end of the document.

The <HEAD> and </HEAD> Tags

The content of a Web page is essentially broken up into two parts: the head and the body. Both parts are encompassed within the <HTML> and </HTML> tags. The head tags contain the document's header information, such as the document title, which is used by Web browsers.

Many search programs restrict themselves to the text within the head tags when performing a search, so it is worth considering carefully what you will enclose within them. For example, many designers include the page title and introductory paragraph as part of the header information, enabling browsers and search programs to quickly access important information about the site.

The <TITLE> and </TITLE> Tags

The <TITLE> and </TITLE> tags are usually placed within the <HEAD> tags. The title you specify within these tags will be displayed in the Web browser's title bar, and on certain Web browsers will also appear in the history list (a hyperlinked record of sites the user has visited).

In addition, when visitors add the Universal Resource Location (URL) of your website to their bookmark file, the text enclosed in the <TITLE> tags will be shown as the bookmark's name.

The <BODY> and </BODY> Tags

The <BODY> and </BODY> tags enclose the actual "body" of your Web page: the text, graphics and links that will be displayed by the viewer's browser. The <BODY> tag is placed immediately after the </HEAD> end tag. The basic outline of a Web page will look similar to the tags shown below (don't worry if you don't recognise all the tags - they will be explained in following sections):

```
<HTML>
<HEAD>
<TITLE>My Sample Web Page</TITLE>
</HEAD>
<BODY>
    <H1>My First Web Page</H1>
    <P>
    This is my first Web page.
    </P>
    <P>
    I think that I have some way to go before I
get the hang of it all!
    </P>
</BODY>
</HTML>
```

When viewed in a Web browser the text and tags appear as:

My First Web Page

This is my first Web page.
I think that I have some way to go before I get the hang of it all!

Tags Tags Used Within the Body of a Document

Heading Tags

Heading tags (not to be confused with the head tags <HEAD> and </HEAD>) are used to emphasise text within an HTML document by changing its size and displaying it in somewhat heavier type.

There are six different heading sizes, numbered 1 to 6, with H1 being the largest. The heading tags are used in pairs. For example:

```
<H1>Heading 1</H1>
<H2>Heading 2</H2>
<H3>Heading 3</H3>
<H4>Heading 4</H4>
<H5>Heading 5</H5>
<H6>Heading 6</H6>
```

When viewed with a Web browser the heading tags and text shown above would appear as shown below:

Heading 1
Heading 2
Heading 3
Heading 4
Heading 5
Heading 6

Each heading appears on its own line, and you can't have two headings on one line.

The Line Break Tag

HTML ignores any carriage returns or extra spaces in your HTML coding. You must explicitly stipulate where you want new lines or blank lines to appear using tags.

To force the next line or word to start on a new line, use the line break tag <BR>. (Note there is no corresponding </BR> tag, as there is really no such thing as the end of a line break!)

The Paragraph Tag

Strictly speaking, each paragraph of text should be enclosed within the paragraph tags <P> and </P>. However, the </P> tag is not required, and few people use it. Each time the paragraph tag appears, it instructs the Web browser to skip a line, so paragraphs have quite a bit of space between them. The paragraph tags can also be used to align text to the left, right or centre of the viewer's screen, by including an ALIGN= statement. The modified tags look like this:

`<P ALIGN=LEFT>`	**aligns paragraph left**
`<P ALIGN=RIGHT>`	**aligns paragraph right**
`<P ALIGN=CENTER>`	**centres paragraph**

Note that HTML requires the American spelling "center".

Blockquote Tags

The blockquote tags (<BLOCKQUOTE> and </BLOCKQUOTE>) indent text, and are used to emphasise quoted text. Blockquote tags can be used in conjunction with other tags, such as the boldface tag, or nested within tags, such as the paragraph tags.

When the blockquote tag is used, the quoted text is placed on a new line (that is, there is an implicit line break).

The List Tags

Lists are fun, and quite handy. They can be used to make points stand out from other text (for example, to summarise the advantages of your products and services).

There are three basic types of lists: ordered, unordered and definition. The first two are quite similar and very easy to use. Definition lists, however, are set up in quite a different fashion.

The Ordered List Tags

Ordered list tags are used in conjunction with text to set up a numbered sequence. The ordered list tags instruct the Web browser to mark each point with an automatically generated, sequential number.

The <OL> tag marks the beginning of the listed items, and the </OL> tag marks the end. Each item in the list is preceded by the <LI> ("list item") tag. The corresponding </LI> tag isn't required. For example, you could use the ordered list tags to itemise the resources on your site:

```
<OL>
<LI>HTML tutorials
<LI>Links to free software
<LI>My favourite sites
<LI>Some fun sites
</OL>
```

> 1 HTML tutorials
>
> 2 Links to free software
>
> 3 My favourite sites
>
> 4 Some fun sites

As the image shows, when the list defined by the HTML is displayed on the user's screen, a sequential number precedes each list item. But why use the ordered list tags when you could simply (and manually) number each item? The reason is that if you want to add extra items to a list which uses ordered list tags, you can simply insert new items and the entire list will be automatically renumbered - a significant time saver.

Unordered Lists

If you use a word processor, you are probably familiar with "bulleted lists", in which each item is placed on a separate line and preceded by a small graphic, such as a circle or diamond. Bulleted lists can be achieved with HTML using the unordered list tags, <UL> and </UL>:

```
<UL>
<LI>HTML tutorials
<LI>Links to free software
<LI>My favourite sites
<LI>Some fun sites
</UL>
```

Instead of article titles being preceded by a number, a "bullet" (most browsers use a small, solid circle) precedes each article, as shown below:

- HTML tutorials
- Links to free software
- My favourite sites
- Some fun sites

Definition lists

This is where things get a little tricky! Definition lists are used to group pairs of text items. For instance, you might want each article title to be followed by a brief description of that article. To do this, you could use the definition list tags: <DL> and </DL> to begin and end the list, <DT> to specify the first item in a pair, and <DD> to specify the second item (or "definition") as in the following example:

```
<DL>
<DT>HTML tutorials
    <DD>Links to some cool online tutorials
<DT>Links to free software
    <DD>Some of the best software around
<DT>My favourite sites
    <DD>Where I like to hang out
<DT>Some fun sites
    <DD>The Web isn't all work with no play
</DL>
```

When viewed with a browser, the tags above would look like this:

HTML tutorials
        Links to some cool online tutorials
Links to free software
        Some of the best software around
My favourite sites
        Where I like to hang out
Some fun sites
        The Web isn't all work with no play

Style Tags

In the same way that you can highlight words in your word processor using underline, boldface and italics, you can change text attributes in HTML using the style tags below.

The Boldface Tags

Everything between the <B> and </B> tags is boldfaced (that is, darkened text).

The Italics Tags

Everything between the tags <I> and </I> tags is italicised.

The Underline Tags

Text enclosed within the <U> and </U> tags is underlined. Be aware, however, that many designers do not use underline tags. Browsers often use underlined text to designate links, and including underlined text that does not function as a link can confuse and frustrate visitors.

The following example uses style tags:

<B>   This section of text should appear in BOLD</B>

<I>   This section of text should appear in ITALICS</I>
<BR
<U>   This section of text should appear UNDERLINED</U>

This example looks like the following image when displayed with a Web browser:

This section of text should appear in BOLD

This section of text should appear in ITALICS

This section of text should appear UNDERLINED

The Font Size and Colour Tags

In addition to using standard text formatting, you can change the size and colour of your text using the <FONT SIZE> and <FONT COLOR> tags. For instance, the <FONT SIZE=4> tag would create text twice as large as the <FONT SIZE=2> tag.

Because the header tags require that header text appear on its own line, many users prefer to create headlines and headings using the <FONT SIZE> tag, which allows them to choose whether or not text will appear on a separate line. Experiment with different size values to get an idea of what you can achieve with font sizes.

To change the colour of displayed text use the <FONT COLOR> tag (note the American spelling of "color"). While there are a large number of possible colours that you can use with this tag, not all are supported by every Web browser. Commonly supported colours are blue, white, cyan, black, fuchsia, and magenta. For example:

```
<FONT COLOR=RED>
```

For a detailed list of font colours for use on the Web, visit www.geocities.com/~annabella/color.html

Note that the closing </FONT> tag is used regardless of the content of the <FONT> tag.

The Horizontal Rules Tag <HR>

Horizontal rules are a handy way of dividing different parts of your HTML document. A horizontal rule is exactly what the name suggests - a ruled "line" across the screen that extends the full width of the browser window.

Creating Links

Most websites include links to related sites, or to other Web pages within the site. These links are generated using anchor tags, which are described overleaf.

Anchor Tags <A> and </A>

The anchor tags are used in conjunction with other commands, which modify their function.

The HREF Command

The most common anchors used are in the form <A HREF="URL">, where URL is the Universal Resource Locator (or Internet address) of the site, document or resource to which you wish to create a link. HREF is an acronym for "Hypertext REFerence".

For example, you might suggest that visitors to your site download the latest copy of your favourite game. You can include a link on your site such as:

```
<A   HREF="http://www.sierra.com/">The   Sierra
website</A>
```

The text between the open and close anchor ("The Sierra website") will be displayed in a different colour or underlined (depending on how the visitor's Web browser is configured) to indicate it is a hyperlink. By clicking on the link visitors will automatically connect to Sierra's home page, where they can download copies of the latest games.

To direct the reader to a new page or HTML document on your own site, use the same command tags, but replace the URL with the directory path and name of the document. For example:

```
<A HREF="nextpage.html">Click here to move to the
next page...</A>
```

Anchor tags can also be used to create a link on your website to your email address, making it easy for visitors to send you email. By inserting a "mailto" command, visitors can click to open their favourite email program with a blank email message already addressed to you. The mailto tag works like this:

```
<A HREF="mailto:your email address">Click here to
send me email</A>
```

For example, if I wanted to include a mailto link on my website, I would use the command:

```
<A   HREF="mailto:mpn@infolution.com.">Click   here
to send me email</A>
```

Linking to a Place on a Web Document

Sometimes websites are set up as a single page, to make printing their contents easier. A recipe book, for example, can have an index at the top of a page, with all the recipes following consecutively.

Rather than requiring readers to scroll through a long Web page (remember, most users won't scroll!), you can insert a series of "anchor" hyperlinks allowing users to jump to particular sections of the document. The tag used to do this is very similar to the hyperlink tag, but instead of pointing to a URL or a separate Web document, the tag points to another tag, the name tag.

In the example of a recipe book, the links at the top of the Web page would contain pointers to the various recipe types. The specific tags might look like this:

```
<A HREF="#start">Starters</A>
<BR>
<A HREF="#entree">Entree</A>
<BR>
<A HREF="#main">Main Meals</A>
<BR>
<A HREF="#dessert">Dessert</A>
<BR>
```

As you can see, these tags point to the areas of the document titled "#start", "#entree" and so on. In the document itself, there would be corresponding tags:

```
<A NAME="start">Starters</A>

<P>Here is a selection of mouth-watering starters
to suit all lifestyles and budgets. The first
section features starters for meat eaters, while
vegetarians are catered for in the following
section. Take your time and enjoy our fabulous
recipes. </P>
[text of recipes]
...
<A NAME="dessert">Dessert </A>
```

Pretty Pictures

Life would be quite boring without colour. Similarly, a website would be fairly unattractive without graphics. HTML has the answer for this, too.

The IMAGE Tag

Like the anchor tags, the <IMG> tag is used in conjunction with other commands. (Unlike the anchor tags, it stands alone: there is no </IMG> end tag.) Primarily, the image tag is used in conjunction with the SRC (source) command, which tells Web browsers where to retrieve the image file for display.

```
<IMG SRC="name of graphic file">
```

For example, if the image file ball.gif is in the same directory as the document that contains the link, your command would look like this:

```
<IMG SRC="ball.gif">
```

Alternatively, if you borrow an image from another site, you can choose to either download and save a copy, or include a link to it in your Web document. In the latter case, you would insert its full URL, such as:

```
<IMG SRC="http://www.test.co.uk/graphic/ball.gif">
```

When the user's Web browser is loading your Web page, it will grab a copy from the other website and include it in yours. One advantage of this approach is that you do not have to save a copy of the image and then upload it to your website. On the other hand, you have no control over the speed of the other website (a slow site will delay the display of the graphic on your website) and you may need to edit your Web pages if the image is removed from the other site. As with the anchor tags, there are a number of other commands you can use in conjunction with the IMG tag to modify its operation.

The ALT Tag

Unfortunately, not every Internet user has access to a Web browser capable of displaying images. Some users only have access to systems that can't display graphics, while others configure their Web browsers not to display images, as this speeds up searching. When users can't see images, an image icon, left, is substituted for the actual image, to indicate that an image would normally occupy the space marked.

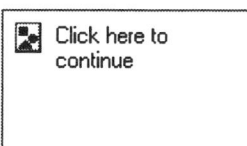

The ALT tag is used to display alternative text for those users who can't, or choose not to, view images. These alternate descriptions are not used or displayed by browsers that can display graphics. For example:

```
<IMG   SRC="arrow.gif"   ALT="Click   Here   to
Continue">
```

The ALIGN Tag

Place the "ALIGN=" tag within the <IMG> tag to align your images on the computer screen. For example:

```
<IMG ALIGN=LEFT SRC="ball.gif">
```

places the image to the far left of the screen.

```
<IMG ALIGN=RIGHT SRC="ball.gif">
```

places the image to the far right of the screen.

```
<IMG ALIGN=CENTER SRC="ball.gif">
```

centres the image.

The HEIGHT and WIDTH Tags

The HEIGHT and WIDTH tags specify the dimension of the image (in pixels). Although it is not compulsory to specify each image's dimensions, it is a good idea to do so, as it helps the visitor's Web browser calculate how much space to leave on the screen for an image that it is yet to download. For example:

```
<IMG SRC="ball.gif" WIDTH=50 HEIGHT=30>
```

If you specify pixel dimensions larger than the actual dimensions of the image, the Web browser will magnify the image. Conversely, if you specify dimensions that are smaller than the actual image, the Web browser will shrink it.

Many Web designers use this to their advantage, purposely creating images that are smaller than necessary (which makes their file sizes smaller, meaning they download faster) then using these tags to "scale" them up.

The VSPACE and HSPACE tags

The VSPACE and HSPACE tags are used to specify the amount of screen space left between an image and the text or image appearing above or below or to the left or right of it. For example:

```
<IMG SRC="ball.gif" VSPACE=50 HSPACE=30>
```

Put them together...

Inserting an image that uses all these features can be tedious, but it is an excellent way of controlling how your image is displayed on screen by a Web browser:

```
<IMG  SRC="ball.gif"  ALIGN=LEFT  ALT="Click  to
proceed  to  the  next  page"  WIDTH=50  HEIGHT=30
VSPACE=10 HSPACE=10>
```

Background Colours

The default background colour for Web pages on most browsers is a light grey, which is practical but not very appealing. Luckily, HTML allows you to change the default colour to something more aesthetically pleasing. You do this by inserting the BGCOLOR="name of colour" command (note the American spelling of "colour") within the <BODY> tag. The modified tag would look something like this:

```
<BODY BGCOLOR="blue">
```

There are quite a few colours that you can use within the <BODY> tag, including blue, yellow, white, red and black.

Background Images

Many people feel the choice of background colours, although broad, is restrictive. To remedy this, HTML allows the use of background images. Instead of using a block of colour as a background, Web pages can display a single image tiled over the page. The background image can be a discernable image, such as a logo or picture of a product. This is a great way of "branding" your Web page. Alternatively, the background image might simply be a special colour or a subtle pattern.

Make sure the background image is not too large, as this will add to the total download "size" of your website. The image should also be subtle enough so visitors can easily read the text. A complex or brightly coloured background image can render a Web page completely illegible.

The command for using background images, which again is inserted within the <BODY> tag, is BACKGROUND="name of image file". For example:

```
<BODY BACKGROUND="logo.gif">
```

Making Comments Within Documents

Occasionally you might want to make comments or leave reminder notes for yourself in an HTML document. For example, you might be rearranging your graphics or trying a new "trick", in which case it's a good idea to leave a message explaining what you are doing for future reference. To insert a comment, use an exclamation point within the tag:

```
<!- This is my comment->
```

The text "This is my comment" will not be displayed on the user's screen.

Tables

Tables can be extremely useful, as they allow authors fairly precise control over how images and text will appear on the page. The table tags were designed to allow information to be displayed in a tabular format (such as spreadsheets, timetables and the like). But users quickly discovered they could also be used to accurately space graphics and text.

Tables can certainly jazz up your Web designs, as they allow for some imaginative page layouts. But be aware - different browsers do interpret some table tags differently. And, when using tables, even minor display variations can change the intended effect.

So, suitably warned, let's take a look at the basic table tags.

Table Tags

Tables are a means of arranging text and images into rows, cells and columns. There are three main tags used to create tables:

Table tags: <TABLE> and </TABLE>
Row tags: <TR> and </TR>
Cell tags: <TD> and </TD>

(Why "TD" to refer to table cells? One school of thought is that it stands for "Table Data", which is what the cells contain.)

The general rule of thumb when it comes to tables is that the tags <TD> and </TD> are used within the tags <TR> and </TR>, which in turn are "wrapped" within the <TABLE> and </TABLE> tags.

When creating a table in HTML it's easiest to first visualise (or draw) the finished table. For example, the image below shows a basic table containing four cells in two rows, creating two columns:

Cell 1 (Row 1)	Cell 2 (Row 1)
Cell 3 (Row 2)	Cell 4 (Row 2)

The HTML commands required to create this basic table are quite straightforward. (Be aware that the following lines of HTML have been indented to make the commands easier to follow on paper. When writing your HTML documents it is not necessary to indent the commands.)

```
<TABLE>
    <TR>
    <TD>Cell 1 (Row 1)</TD>
    <TD>Cell 2 (Row 1)</TD>
    </TR>
    <TR>
    <TD>Cell 3 (Row 2)</TD>
    <TD>Cell 4 (Row 2)</TD>
    </TR>
</TABLE>
```

The data that appears in individual cells is encapsulated within the <TD> tags, which are themselves encapsulated within the individual <TR> tags.

To ensure your table stands out on screen, use borders to insert lines between each row, column and cell. To add a border, use the BORDER= tag within the <TABLE> tag. Default border thickness is indicated by BORDER=1. To vary the border width, simply increase the table border value. For example:

```
<TABLE BORDER=3>
  or
<TABLE BORDER=5>
```

To omit borders, set BORDER=0.

```
<TABLE BORDER=0>
```

Let's have a look at a different style of table (this time one which consists of two rows and three columns):

```
<TABLE BORDER=3>
<CAPTION>A simple table</CAPTION>
    <TR>
  <TH>Column 1</TH>
  <TH>Column 2</TH>
  <TH>Column 3</TH>
    </TR>
    <TR>
  <TD>Number One</TD>
  <TD>Number Two</TD>
  <TD>Number Three</TD>
    </TR>
</TABLE>
```

A simple table

Column 1	Column 2	Column 3
Number One	Number Two	Number Three

You will notice we used a new tag - <TH>. Essentially this works in the same way as the <TD> tab, except that the encapsulated text is treated as a heading (and therefore is displayed in bold).

Another way to make text stand out within your table is to use the <CAPTION> tag, which allows you to attach a descriptive comment to your table.

The example below demonstrates how to create a Web document that consists entirely of a single table.

```
<HTML>
<HEAD>
<TITLE>Roster for School Canteen</TITLE>
</HEAD>
<BODY>
<TABLE BORDER=2>
<CAPTION>Canteen Roster, Week Ending 17.4.01
</CAPTION>
    <TR>
   <TH> <BR> </TH>
   <TH>Monday</TH>
   <TH>Tuesday</TH>
   <TH>Wednesday</TH>
   <TH>Thursday</TH>
   <TH>Friday</TH>
    </TR>
    <TR>
   <TH>8am</TH>
   <TD>Mary</TD>
   <TD>Tanya</TD>
   <TD>Rebekah</TD>
   <TD>Peta</TD>
   <TD>Raegan</TD>
    </TR>
    <TR>
   <TH>10am</TH>
   <TD>Tanya</TD>
   <TD>Rebekah</TD>
   <TD>Peta</TD>
   <TD>Raegan</TD>
   <TD>Mary</TD>
    </TR>
    <TR>
```

```
    <TH>12pm</TH>
    <TD>Rebekah</TD>
    <TD>Peta</TD>
    <TD>Raegan</TD>
    <TD>Mary</TD>
    <TD>Tanya</TD>
      </TR>
</TABLE>
</BODY>
</HTML>
```

This table is shown below.

Canteen Roster, Week Ending 17.4.01

	Monday	Tuesday	Wednesday	Thursday	Friday
8am	Mary	Tanya	Rebekah	Peta	Raegan
10am	Tanya	Rebekah	Peta	Raegan	Mary
12pm	Rebekah	Peta	Raegan	Mary	Tanya

Special Attributes of Tables

Although we have covered the basics of tables in the examples already shown, there are still further refinements possible. For instance, if you only want your table to fill part of the screen, you can control its width and height with the WIDTH=x and HEIGHT=x attributes (set within the <TABLE> tag), where x is measured in pixels.

The width and height attributes can be used in conjunction with other attributes, including BORDER=x, which, as we mentioned earlier, sets the thickness of the table's borders. The following example shows how these tags can be used. Example:

```
<TABLE WIDTH=400 BORDER=5>
<CAPTION>A simple table</CAPTION>
    <TR>
    <TH>Column 1</TH>
    <TH>Column 2</TH>
    <TH>Column 3</TH>
    </TR>
```

```
   <TR>
   <TD>Number One</TD>
   <TD>Number Two</TD>
   <TD>Number Three</TD>
    </TR>
</TABLE>
```

A simple table

Column 1	Column 2	Column 3
Number One	Number Two	Number Three

You can also use the WIDTH= attribute to create columns of varying sizes, as shown in the following example.

```
<TABLE BORDER=3>
<CAPTION>A simple table</CAPTION>
    <TR>
    <TH WIDTH=120>Column 1</TH>
    <TH WIDTH=200>Column 2'</TH>
    <TH WIDTH=60>Column 3</TH>
     </TR>
     <TR>
    <TD>Number One</TD>
    <TD>Number Two</TD>
    <TD>Number Three</TD>
     </TR>
</TABLE>
```

A simple table

Column 1	Column 2	Column 3
Number One	Number Two	Number Three

In addition to determining the perimeter of your table, you can control the spacing between each cell, as well as the space between a cell's content (that is, text or image) and the inner frame of the cell. These effects are achieved by using the CELLSPACING=x and CELLPADDING=x attributes within the <TABLE> tag. Example:

```
<TABLE CELLSPACING=10 BORDER=3>
<CAPTION>A simple table</CAPTION>
    <TR>
    <TH>Column 1</TH>
    <TH>Column 2</TH>
    <TH>Column 3</TH>
     </TR>
     <TR>
    <TD>Number One</TD>
    <TD>Number Two</TD>
    <TD>Number Three</TD>
     </TR>
</TABLE>
```

A simple table

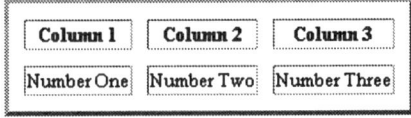

For example:

```
<TABLE CELLPADDING=20 BORDER=3>
<CAPTION>A simple table</CAPTION>
    <TR>
    <TH>Column 1</TH>
    <TH>Column 2</TH>
    <TH>Column 3</TH>
     </TR>
     <TR>
    <TD>Number One</TD>
    <TD>Number Two</TD>
    <TD>Number Three</TD>
     </TR>
</TABLE>
```

A simple table

Column 1	Column 2	Column 3
Number One	Number Two	Number Three

You can also position your table in a specific position on the screen using the ALIGN= attributes. The main attribute settings are "left", "right" and "center". To centre the whole table use the <CENTER> and </CENTER> tags before you start the table (as shown in the example below).

Finally, you can also specify the alignment of data within a cell, using the ALIGN= attribute within the <TD> or <TH> tags (in conjunction with the "left", "right" or "center" settings). You can also use VALIGN=, in conjunction with the "top", "middle" and "bottom" settings, to control the vertical alignment of text.

Example:

```
<CENTER>
<TABLE WIDTH=400 HEIGHT=100 BORDER=4>
<CAPTION>A simple table</CAPTION>
    <TR>
    <TH ALIGN=right>Column 1</TH>
    <TH ALIGN=center>Column 2</TH>
    <TH ALIGN=left>Column 3</TH>
    </TR>
    <TR>
    <TD ALIGN=right VALIGN=top>Number
One</TD>
    <TD ALIGN=center VALIGN=middle>Number
Two</TD>
    <TD ALIGN=left VALIGN=bottom>Number
Three</TD>
    </TR>
</TABLE>
</CENTER>
```

A simple table

Column 1	Column 2	Column 3
Number One	Number Two	Number Three

There are a number of other attributes and tags available for use with tables, most of which you will find in the resources listed below.

Resources

WebMonkey Tutorials	www.webmonkey.com
HTML Primer	www.htmlprimer.com
Guide to HTML & Forms	www.2kweb.net/
Interactive HTML Tutorial	www.davesite.com/webstation/html/
Builders	www.builders.com
Quadzilla	www.quadzilla.com
Simple Builder	www.xpertz.com/builder/
HitBox Web Resources	resources.hitbox.com

Chapter 7

HTML Examples

In the previous chapter, we looked at the basic HTML tags you are likely to use if you are "hand-coding" your first Web page. While the preceding chapter is a handy ready-reference, you won't really get a feel for how HTML works until you see several actual Web documents, and start picking them apart. In this chapter, we've created a series of basic Web pages, which are displayed both in their raw HTML format and as screenshots so you can see how they appear when viewed with a Web browser. Each document is accompanied by a running commentary (inserted within an exclamation point within a tag, in the same way you can leave notes for yourself within an HTML document), to help you make sense of it all.

A handy "trick" is to use your Web browser to look at the HTML code of any website. For example, in Internet Explorer 5, select Source from the View pull-down menu and the raw HTML of the Web page you are currently viewing will be displayed in a separate window. This will help you learn new tricks, and provide "live" examples of how other people structure their Web pages.

A "Favourite Links" Website

Many people use their first attempt at Web authoring to create a website containing a list of their favourite Web resources for their friends and online associates. These types of websites are very easy to create, as you will soon see.

Over the page is the HTML code for a fictitious website,

Hint

If you really want to impress other internet users, and keep them coming back, place less emphasis on snazzy web deign and pay more attention to creating original, interesting content.

called Lucy's Web Page. For ease of commentary, we have put each tag on a separate line. However, Web browsers do not recognise standard line breaks (only those inserted with the <BR> tag), so it wouldn't matter if you used more than one tag on a line, as shown below:

```
<FONT SIZE=3> <B>Software Links</B>
</FONT SIZE>
```

You could even place all of the tags below for Lucy's Web Page on a single line!

```
<HTML>
<HEAD>
<TITLE>Lucy's Web Page</TITLE>
</HEAD>
<!- Here we are specifying colours throughout the
document->
<BODY BGCOLOR="Black" TEXT="White" LINK="Teal">
<CENTER>
<P>
<FONT SIZE=5 COLOR="Fuchsia">
<IMG SRC="squiggle.gif">
<!- We are creating extra space between the pic
and the text by making our text the same colour
as the background, therefore making it unreadable
to users. This is a trick that can be used as an
alternative to the <P> tag->
<FONT COLOR="Black">aaaaaaaa</FONT COLOR>
<B>Hi!</B>
<FONT COLOR="Black">aaaaaaaa</FONT COLOR>
<FONT COLOR="Black">This text will be the same
colour as the background, and therefore won't be
legible</FONT COLOR>
<IMG SRC="squiggle.gif">
<BR>
My name is <B>Lucy</B>
<BR>
and this is my web page of favourite links.</FONT>
```

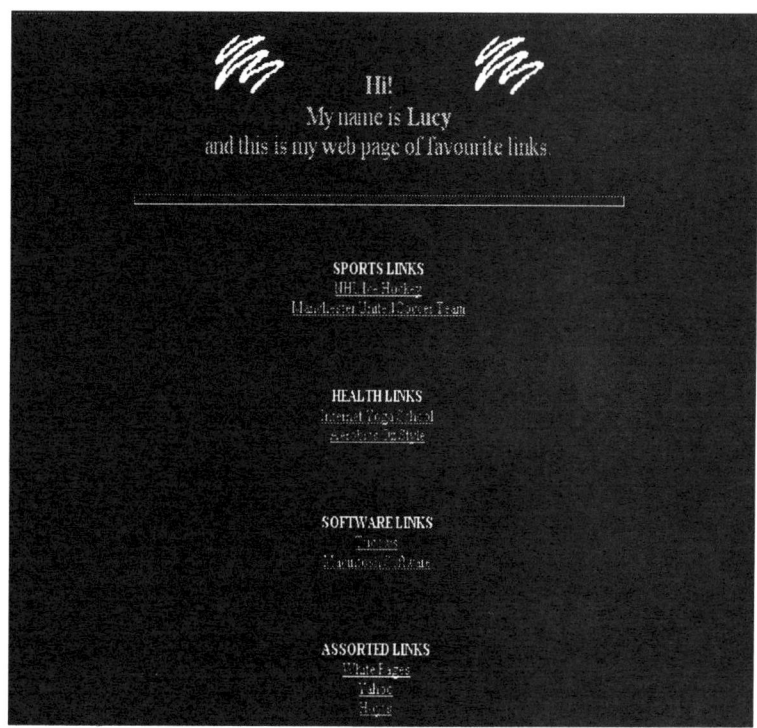

How Lucy's webpage looks through the eyes of a web browser.

```
<HR width=50% size=8>
<P>
<FONT SIZE=3>
<B>SPORTS LINKS</B>
</FONT>
<BR>
<A HREF="http://www.nhl.com/">
NHL Ice Hockey
</A>
<BR>
<A HREF="http://www.sky.co.uk/manu/">
Manchester United Soccer Team</A>
<P>
<FONT SIZE=3>
<B>HEALTH LINKS</B>
```

```
</FONT>
<BR>
<A HREF="http://www.charliechan.com.uk/fran. html">
Internet Yoga School</A>
<BR>
<A HREF="http://www.zero1zero.com.uk/AOS/index.asp">
Aerobics Oz Style</A>
<P>
<FONT SIZE=3>
<B>SOFTWARE LINKS</B>
</FONT>
<BR>
<A HREF="http://tucows.ideal.net.uk/">
Tucows</A>
<BR>
<A HREF="http://tucows.ideal.net.uk/mac/mac
intosh.html">
Macintosh Software</A>
<P>
<FONT SIZE=3>
<B>ASSORTED LINKS</B>
</FONT>
<BR>
<A HREF="http://www.whitepages.com.uk">
White Pages</A>
<BR>
<A HREF="http://www.yahoo.com">
Yahoo </A>
<BR>
<A HREF="http://www.hoyts.com.au">
Hoyts</A>
</CENTER>
</BODY>
</HTML>
```

Create a clean, fresh layout with the minimum of fuss using tables

A Basic Small Business Web Page

The following layout for Julie's Bakery demonstrates how to use the table tags to format a Web page layout. The Web page contains a mailto: link so visitors can contact Julie's staff instantly with orders or requests for further information. If this were a "live" site, the bulleted list could be displayed as hyperlinks, with links to other sections of the website containing images of the product and prices.

```
<HTML>
<HEAD>
<TITLE>Julie's Bakery</TITLE>
</HEAD>
<BODY BGCOLOR="White">
<!-The table forms the basis of our page layout.
All images and text are contained within table
elements->
<TABLE CELLPADDING=10 BORDER=0>
<TR VALIGN=top>
<TD> <IMG SRC="bread.jpg" WIDTH=150>
</TD>
<TD> <BR> <IMG SRC="julie.gif" WIDTH=350> </TD>
```

```
</TR>
<TR VALIGN=top>
<TD> <BR> <IMG SRC="cakes.jpg" WIDTH=150><BR>
<IMG SRC="cookies.jpg" WIDTH=150> </TD>
<TD> <BR> <B>MISSION STATEMENT</B> <BR>
Julie's Bakery aims to provide our customers with
the finest, freshest food.<BR> We aim to satisfy
even the fussiest of tastebuds and offer a full
guarantee of quality on all our food. <P>
<B><I>Satisfaction or your money back!</I></B>
<P>Just a small selection of the tasty treats we
offer are:
<!-Since the following is an unordered list,
there is no need to close the <LI> tag->
<UL>
<LI>Fresh Bread and Scones
<LI>Chocolate Mud Cakes
<LI>Pastries - Sweet; Custard Tarts, Matchsticks
etc.
<LI>Pastries - Savoury; Pies, Sausage Rolls,
Pasties etc.
<LI>Cakes for all Occasions
</UL>
<P>
<CENTER>
<I>Thankyou for visiting our site</I>
<P>
<!-The tags below provide browsers with the
opportunity to email directly from the site->
This site is maintained and updated by <A
HREF="mailto:juliesbakery@bakers.com">Julie
</A> <BR>
Last modified 30th May, 2001.
</CENTER>
</TD>
</TR>
</TABLE>
</BODY>
</HTML>
```

Small Car Enthusiasts' Website

The site shown below features a modest main graphic on the opening screen, some text and four navigational icons. Again, it is a fairly simple site. The page aims to welcome visitors and direct them to specific areas of interest within the site. At the bottom of the screen is an invitation to visitors to contact the site's owner with any questions or queries.

```
<HTML>
<HEAD>
<TITLE>Pedal to the Metal</TITLE>
</HEAD>
<BODY background="ripple.gif" text="Black">
<P>
<CENTER>
```

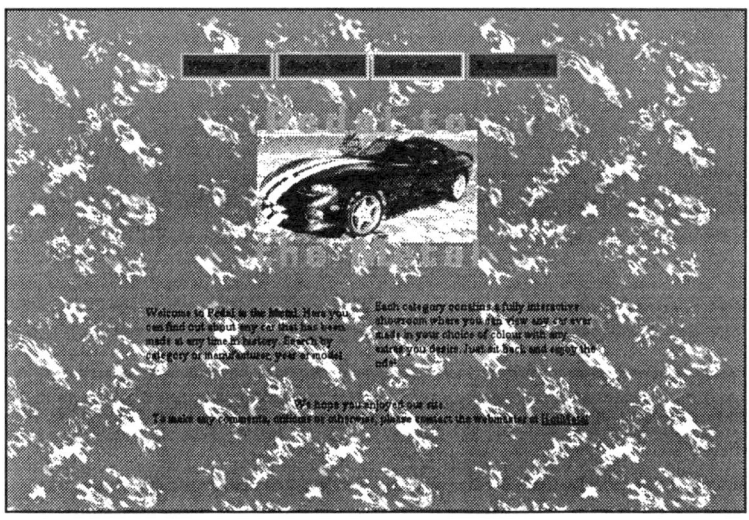

```
<A HREF="vintage.htm">
<IMG SRC="vintage.gif" WIDTH=100 BORDER=0> </A>
<A HREF="sports.htm">
<IMG SRC="sports.gif" WIDTH=100 BORDER=0> </A>
<A HREF="fast.htm">
<IMG SRC="fast.gif" WIDTH=100 BORDER=0> </A>
<A HREF="racing.htm">
<IMG SRC="racing.gif" WIDTH=100 BORDER=0> </A>
<P>
<IMG SRC="97viper.gif" WIDTH=250>
<P>
<!-We use a table to create two columns of text-
>
<TABLE WIDTH=500 BORDER=0 CELLPADDING=5>
<TR>
<TD>Welcome to <B>Pedal to the Metal</B>. Here
you can find out about any car that has been made
at any time in history. Search by category or
manufacturer, year or model.</TD>
<TD>Each category contains a fully interactive
showroom where you can view any car ever made in
your choice of colour with any extras you desire.
Just sit back and enjoy the ride!</TD>
<TR>
</TABLE>
<P>We hope you enjoyed our site.<BR>
<!-Below visitors can email the website owner->
To make any comments, criticisms or otherwise,
please contact the webmaster at
<A HREF="mailto:pedalmetal@hotmetal.com.au">
HotMetal</A>
</FONT>
</CENTER>
</BODY>
</HTML>
```

Chapter 8

Web Authoring Programs

In Chapter 6 we examined the basic structure of HTML and the types of tags new users are likely to enlist when creating their first website. As you can see from the resources listed at the end of the chapter, there is a lot more to HTML than simply the basic tags we discussed.

Thankfully, users need no longer acquaint themselves with the ins and outs of every HTML tag before being in a position to create professional-looking and interesting websites. There are now a number of point-and-click, so-called "WYSIWYG" ("what you see is what you get") Web authoring programs that allow you to manipulate text and graphics within a Web document without worrying about the underlying HTML.

Want to insert an image? Simply open the appropriate menu, select the image you want and point your mouse to the position you want it placed. Want to use a different font size or style? Highlight the text to be changed and select the desired style from a menu. All the relevant options and functions are available via menus and toolbars and during the processes of creation and editing, your Web page is displayed exactly as it would appear in a Web browser. In this chapter we will look at one of the user-friendliest Web authoring programs available: ixla Web Easy.

ixla Web Easy

ixla Web Easy is a fully-featured Web authoring program designed for beginner and intermediate Web authors. Using ixla you can create dynamic, professional-looking sites by selecting a "template" site and adding your own text and images. Or, you can let the Web Assistant guide you through the process of creating your website.

The CD-ROM that accompanies this guide features a free "lite" version of ixla Web Easy. It is not "crippled" in any way, nor is it time-limited, so you can start creating websites immediately and continue using the software for as long as you want.

The "lite" version does not, however, feature all the website templates available in the full version, nor does it have the full range of Web-ready images (the retail version features more than 50,000 ready-to-use images).

To upgrade to the retail version of ixla Web Easy, visit ixla's website at www.ixla.com

> ### Hint
>
> Before you can add photographs to your site you will need to convert them to image files using a digital scanner. Alternatively, take photos with a digital camera, then load them onto your pc

Launching ixla Web Easy

Once installed, you can launch Web Easy by selecting the program from the ixla Web Easy program group or by double-clicking on the ixla Web Easy desktop icon (if you chose to install one during the installation process).

Web Easy will launch and then display the main Web Easy editing window. Inside this window you will see the Activity Guide dialog box, see below.

The Activity Guide offers several options. These include accessing Web Easy's step-by-step, interactive tutorials, opening

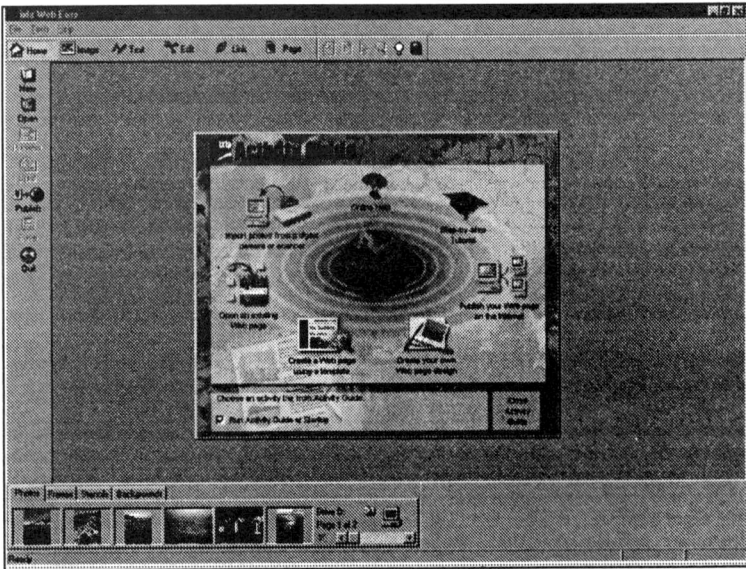

an existing Web page (if you have already created one in a previous session or using another Web authoring program) or publishing your existing Web pages.

Creating a Website

For beginners, the most important option in the Activity Guide dialog box is labelled "Create a Web page using a template". Select this option by clicking once on it and the website Assistant appears, ready to guide you through each step involved in creating a website.

Click the Next button to get started. Once you have finished each website Assistant step, click the Next button to move to the next screen. (You can use the Back button to return to previous screens and modify your preferences.) The first step in the

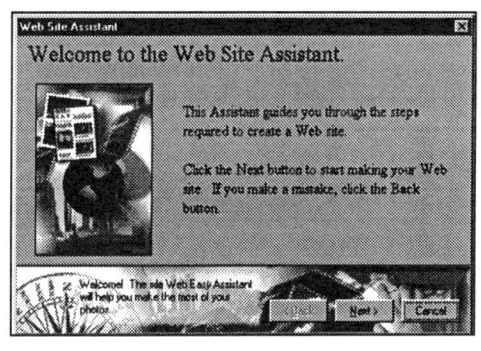

process is to select a suitable template. Generic personal and business websites, plus a range of "themed" templates are offered.

For those designing a business website, there are many different business-style templates available, including Modern Corporate, Bookstore and Art Gallery. If you are designing a family website, you'll find several templates to choose from, including a Family Tree site for mapping out relatives and ancestors. If you plan to use your website to publish information about your favourite hobby, actor, band or sport, use one of the "Info" templates offered. Ranges of kids' websites and personal website templates are also offered.

To learn more about a particular template, highlight it by clicking on it once. The site's "stats", including how many pages it includes and the number of photos you can insert in it are displayed to the right of the temp-late list. A preview of each individual page is also displayed, so you can get an idea of the look and feel of the site.

For the purposes of this example, we'll choose the generic Personal website template. Highlight the template by clicking once on its name, then click on the Next button.

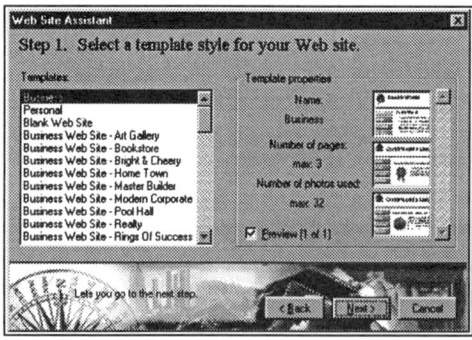

You are then prompted to supply a name for your website as well as specify the folder where you would like to store the files created during the editing process. If you plan to create a number of different websites, you may like to give each site its own folder. Otherwise you can store your

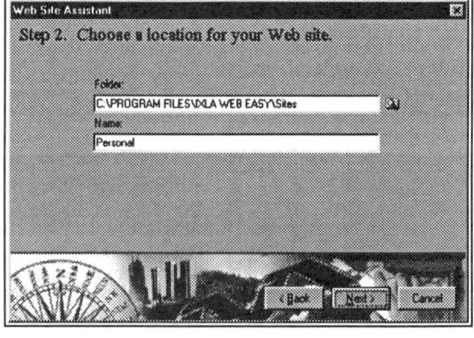

website in the default folder suggested by the website Assistant.

 To select a specific folder, click the folder icon next to the Folder textbox.

You will then be prompted to select or create a new folder.

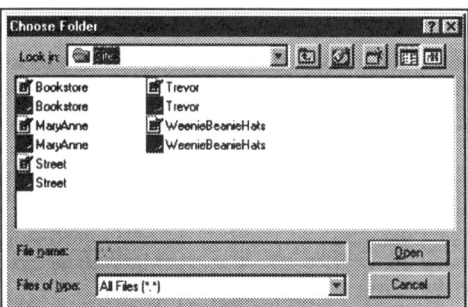

Next, the website Assistant prompts you for personal contact details. Provision is made for entering your name, street address, email address, city, country and postcode details. As websites are generally publicly available - anyone can visit and view your website - you may wish to omit your street address, or provide a postal address instead.

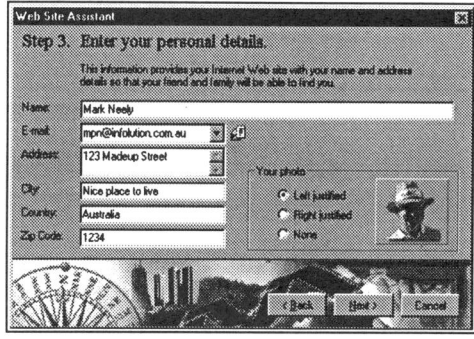

To add your picture to the Web page, click once on the default photo shown on-screen. The Choose Image dialog box will appear.

Use this dialog box to locate the image file you want to insert. You must also choose where on the page you want to place your personal photo. If you don't want to display a photo on the site click inside the radio button labelled "None".

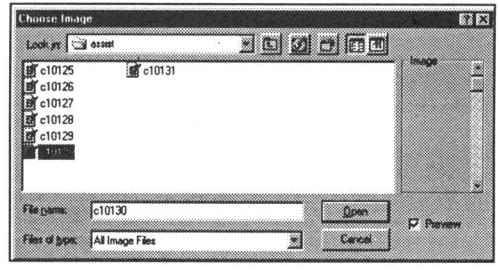

On the next screen you are prompted for information about yourself. The website Assistant asks several questions (such as what your favourite movie is and why you like the Internet), and even provides a range of default answers to choose from. You can, of course, enter your own answers.

The next two screens ask for more personal information, including your hair colour and favourite hobby. Enter the relevant information, or leave the textboxes blank.

On the next screen you can add any extra information you wish to include on your home page. Each additional piece of information is called a "story". To add a story, enter it in the Description textbox, then enter a title in the Title textbox. Click on the button featuring double arrows (displayed at the top of the sequence of arrows) to add the story to the list of stories.

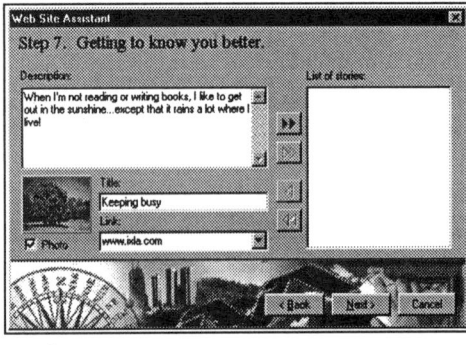

To display an image or photo with your stories click on the photo in the lower left-hand corner of the screen. The Choose Image dialog box appears. Follow the prompts to select the correct image.

On the next screen -Step 8 - you can add the addresses and descriptions of favourite websites you want to share with visitors.

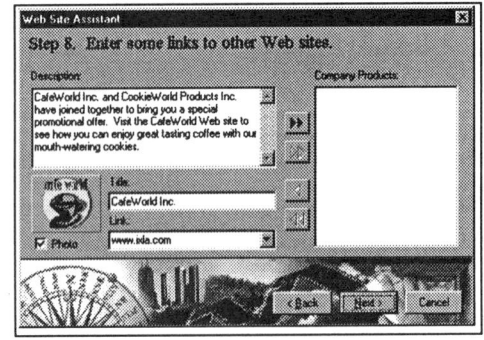

Enter the description in the Description text-box, the name of the website in the Title textbox and its Web address (URL) in the Link textbox. To add the site to your list, click on the button displaying double arrows. Repeat this process to add links to other sites.

Step 9 allows you to choose the colour theme which will be used throughout your website, including the background colour or image, a personal logo and the colour used to display hyperlinks (that is, links to other websites and to the pages within your website).

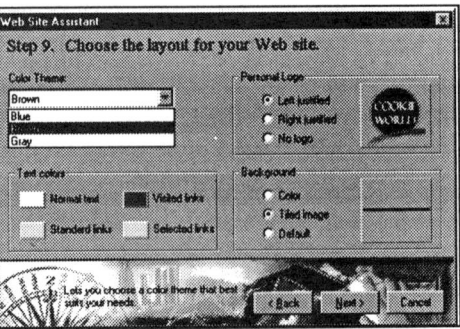

To select a scheme, click on the downward pointing arrow in the Color Theme section and choose a colour from the pull-down menu. To add a personal logo, click on the image in the Personal Logo section to display the Choose Image dialog box, then select your preferred image. To align your image to the left or right of the page select a radio button in this section.

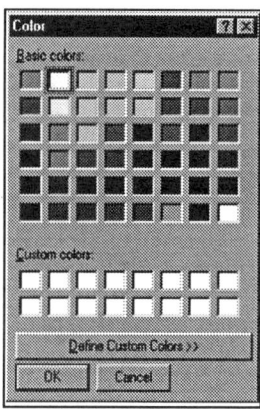

To specify a colour for hyperlinks, click on a box in the section marked "Text colors". The Color dialog box will appear displaying a colour palette. To select a colour click on it once, then click the OK button.

You have three choices of back-grounds for your website. You can choose to use a single colour, tile a small image or apply the default grey look. To select a background, click on a radio button in the Background section. If you have chosen to use an image or colour, you will then need to select an option from the box at the right of the Background section. Once you have made all your selections from this screen, click on the Next button.

From the final screen you can instruct the Assistant to generate your website. To do this, the Assistant will modify the template you selected using the options you chose and the information supplied.

To create your new site, click inside the checkbox labelled "Generate website now", then click on the Finish button. Within a few seconds, the first page of your new website will be displayed on-screen, exactly as it will look in a browser, see over.

Use the scroll bar to examine the page, checking for any spelling errors or other problems. To view the next page(s), click on the "Display the next page" toolbar button, left.

Modifying your Website

If the site or individual pages are not exactly as you envisaged them, you can choose to edit or change your website. To edit text, simply double-click on it. The text will be displayed against a whité back-

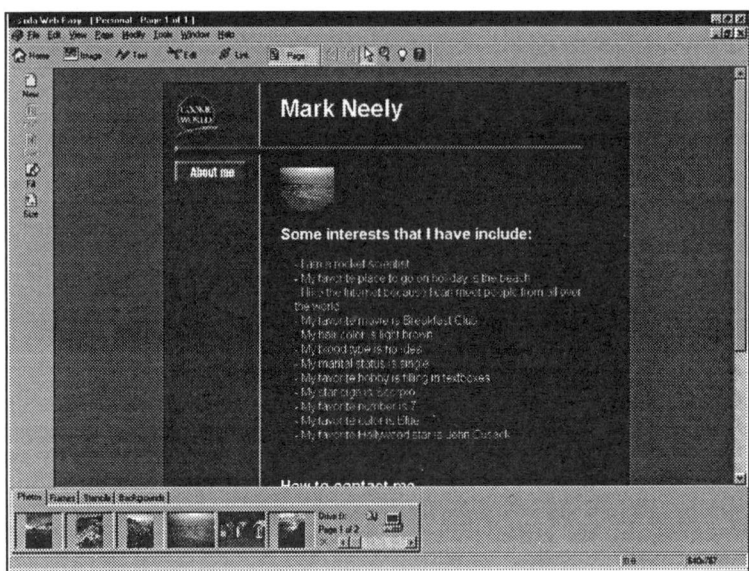

ground, ready for editing. Once you have finished editing the text, click once on another region of the page to confirm the changes.

To reposition an image, click on it once to highlight it (a frame appears around the highlighted image), then click and drag it into position. To resize an image, click on it once to highlight it, then click on one of the small boxes on the frame (known as a "resize handle"). Drag the resize handle to the left or right to change the image size. You can also use this process to reposition or resize buttons and other page elements, as well as to move and change the shape of a section of text.

To manipulate text, click once on the text to display the frame and resize handles. To reposition the text, click on the frame and, while holding down your left mouse button, drag the frame to the new position on screen. To increase or decrease the area occupied by the text, drag a resize handle to the left or right.

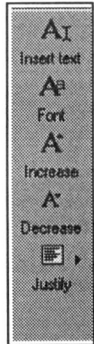

Additional editing tools are available along the left-hand side of the screen and are activated when you select an image or section of text. For instance, when you click on a section of text you can choose to increase or decrease its size, change the font used, or modify the text alignment.

When you select an image, the Image tools are activated. These allow you to apply image effects (such as altering the brightness and contrast of an image), offer a range of frames which you can place around the image, and allow you to rotate and "flip" the image.

Saving the Finished Product

Once you have finished reworking your text, adding or changing the images, or just playing with the range of editing options, you can access a list of "administrative" functions by clicking on the Home button at the far left of the toolbar. A menu appears along the left side of the screen offering a number of options. These options are described below:

- **New:**
  Create a new website with the website Assistant.

- **Open:**
  Open one of the websites that you've already created.

- **Preview:**
  Preview the website that you are currently editing in your default Web browser.

- **Build:**
  Save the website that you have designed as HTML files (that is, the files that you can upload to a website).

- **Publish:**
  Launch the Publishing Assistant, which will take you through the process of uploading your pages to the Web server that will be hosting your website (normally your ISP's Web server).

- **Save:**
  Saves a copy of the website you are working on. (This option does not create Internet-ready files.

You must use the Build option to generate files ready to upload.)

- **Close:**
  Closes the current website.

As you never know when computer malfunctions might occur, it's always prudent to save your Web documents from time to time as you work on them.

As mentioned above, Web Easy's Save function creates a copy of your website in its own file "format" (in much the same way as, say, Microsoft Word uses its own internal format (.doc) to save word processing files). Files saved in this format are not ready to be uploaded to your website. To create Web-ready files, you must use the Build function, which we will now look at in detail.

"Building" Your Website

After you have finished editing your Web pages, and before you can upload it to the computer that will be hosting your website, you need to "build" the HTML files which comprise the site you have just designed. To do this, select the Build option, either from the Home menu or by selecting Build from the File pull-down menu.

The Build Internet website dialog box appears. Here you will specify a separate directory in which to store your HTML files. To do this, either accept the default folder, or click the folder icon to specify a location.

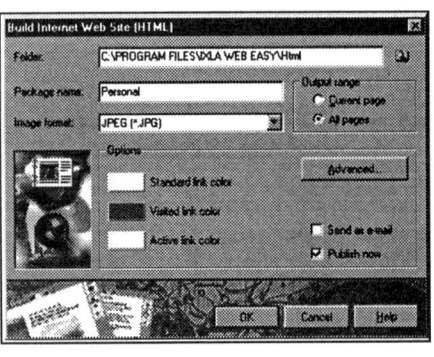

Note that it's generally a good idea to create a new folder for each different website.

The Package name and Image format options can be left as they are. Ensure that the "All pages" radio button is selected in the Output range section. You are also given the chance to make last minute changes to the colours used to display hyperlinks.

Click on the Advanced button to display the Advanced website Options dialog box.

Here you can edit the meta tags in your HTML files to make your web-site easier for Search Engines to index, by modifying the text in the textbox labelled "Internet search engine keywords". The textbox labelled "Status bar message" allows you to enter text that will scroll along

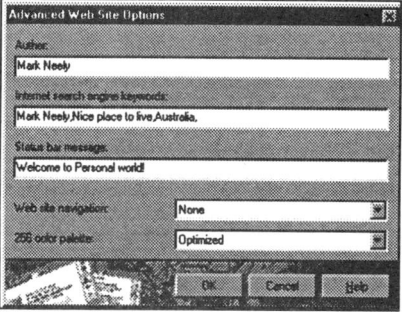

the status bar at the bottom of the visitor's Web browser window while they are viewing your site. Many users find such messages quite annoying, so it's best to leave this box blank.

Click OK to close the dialog box.

Once you have made all the necessary changes within the Build Internet website dialog box, ensure the checkbox labelled "Publish now" is selected, then click OK. Web Easy will generate the necessary HTML files (this may take a few seconds) and auto- matically launch the Publish Assistant, which will take you through the process of uploading your new

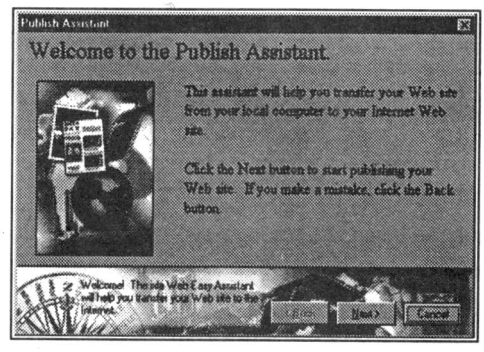

website to the Web server that will be hosting it. Click the Next button to start the Publish Assistant.

Publish Assistant

Click the Connect button and the Connection Profile dialog box appears, prompting you for the details of the Web server that will be hosting your website. This may be your ISP's Web server (if you are taking advantage of the free Web space offered by most ISPs) or one of the various free or inexpensive Web-hosting services. The required details include the address of the Web server, the username and password. Contact your ISP or Web hosting service if you are unsure of these details.

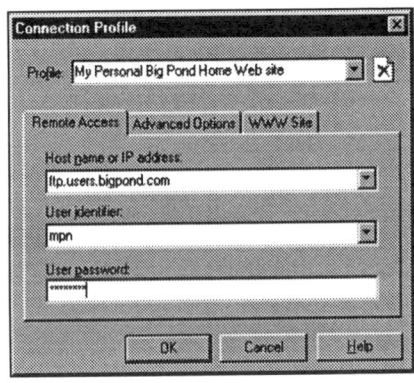

Click on the Advanced Options tab and a textbox will appear in which you can enter the complete address of your website. This may or may not be the same address you use when uploading your website files. (You will need to contact your ISP/Web host about this.) You don't have to enter this address, but if you do, the Publish Assistant will automatically launch your site in your Web browser once it is successfully uploaded, so you can check the process went smoothly.

Click the OK button to connect to the Web server. Once Web Easy has successfully logged in, you will see a confirmation message.

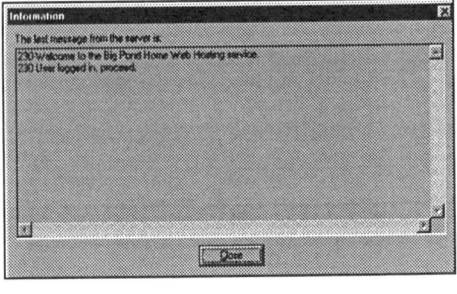

You will then be prompted to choose which websites you wish to upload. (If this is the first website you have created with Web Easy there will only be one web-site package listed.) Highlight the website in the list by clicking on it once, then click Next.

The Publish Assistant will show a final screen confirming the options it will use to upload the website. The default options should suit most users, so you can leave them unchanged.

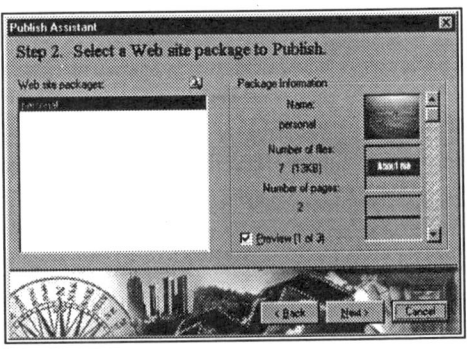

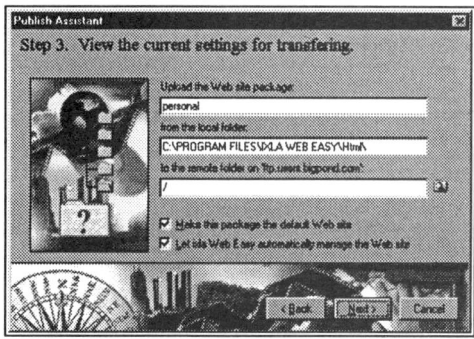

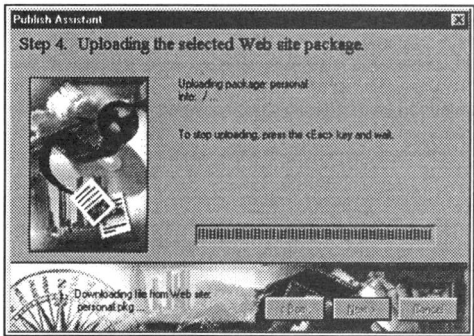

Click the Next button to begin uploading your site to the Web server. This may take a few minutes, depending on the number and size of the photos and images used.

If the upload is successful, the following dialog box appears:

Ensure both checkboxes are selected, then click Finish to view a report of the upload process. Your website should now be uploaded and "live" on the Web!

If you configured the full Web address of your new website in the Advanced Options tab of the Connection Profile dialog box, the Publish Assistant will automatically launch your Web browser and connect to your website. If not, open your Web browser and enter your site address in the address bar, then press the Enter key.

To Frame or not to Frame?

Frames were developed to allow Web designers to "carve" the screen into two or more sections, and then design and code each section individually.

Frames are generally used for navigational or advertising purposes. For example, a narrow frame positioned down the side of the screen might display banner ads constantly, while the remainder of the screen changes depending on which areas of the Website the visitor explores.

The authors are of the view that frames make for poor Web design, and as such do not cover them in this book.

Reasons why you should not use frames include:

- They create unnecessary complexity (both in terms of designing the website and navigating around it).

- They can occasionally alter the user's web browser preferences, especially in terms of image-loading.

- They cause the Web page loading time to appear to be longer (and can add to the download time, as the Wen browser has to download two or more HTML files at a time to create a single screen of information).

- Frames are not universally supported, and many frames implementations are browser-specific.

- Finally, if these are not reason enough to avoid frames, then perhaps the fact that most users hate them will convince you!

Chapter 9

Publishing your Website

If you have designed your website using a Web authoring program that doesn't feature a built-in upload utility, or if you have composed your files using HTML, you will need to upload them with an FTP program.

Once your website files have been uploaded to the Web server (which, in most cases, is your Internet Service Provider's Web server), the site becomes publicly viewable - that is, anyone can connect to your website and view it, as long as they know its URL.

What you Need
In order to upload your website, you need the following:

- Details of the Web server and directory to which you must upload the files (your Internet Service Provider (ISP), or the organisation providing your space on a Web server, will give you this information).

- An FTP (short for "file transfer protocol") program to move files to and from your website.

Web Server
Most ISPs give their users (free of charge) space on their Web servers with which to host a website. Generally, you must connect to your ISP's Web server, log in using your userid and password, then upload your Web files to a specific directory. Your ISP should provide you with information on how to do this. You will need to know:

- The Internet address of the Web server (or other host machine) to which you should connect.

- The procedure required to log on.

- Whether you need to create a special directory to store your Web files (and, if so, what you should call that directory).

- Whether you need to give your website files specific names or file extensions.

Several ISPs now make the process of configuring your Internet account for Web hosting a breeze. They provide special "wizards" on their websites that create any special directory or files needed on the Web server to get your website up and running. It's then just a simple matter of uploading your files to the Server.

If your ISP won't allow users to store Web pages on the Web server, you may want to contact one of the Web-hosting services listed in the resources section at the end of this chapter.

File Transfer Programs

FTP ("file transfer protocol") is the Internet protocol that regulates how files are transferred across the Internet. There are many FTP programs available. Two of the most popular Windows programs are WS_FTP and CuteFTP, while for Macintosh users, Anarchie and Fetch lead the pack. Details of where you can download these programs are at the end of this chapter.

Many Web authoring programs designed for beginners include a built-in FTP capability, so you can use the same software to create and upload your Web pages. This means you only have to configure the software once, and allows you to make updates to your pages whenever necessary.

Hint

Avoid cool tricks and glitzy effects - even if they are temptingly easy to create. Many Web authoring programmes have wizards that automate the process of adding effects to your Website, including flashing and scrolling text. Unless you have a specific reason for using these effects, avoid them. They might look interesting the first time you use them, but most visitors will find them tedious!

The example in this chapter uses WS_FTP. However, the basic elements of FTP programs are fairly standard, and the concepts you learn in this example will be applicable to most FTP programs.

Creating a Session Profile

Once you have installed WS_FTP, start the program by clicking on its icon. WS_FTP will run, displaying the default Session Properties window (see below).

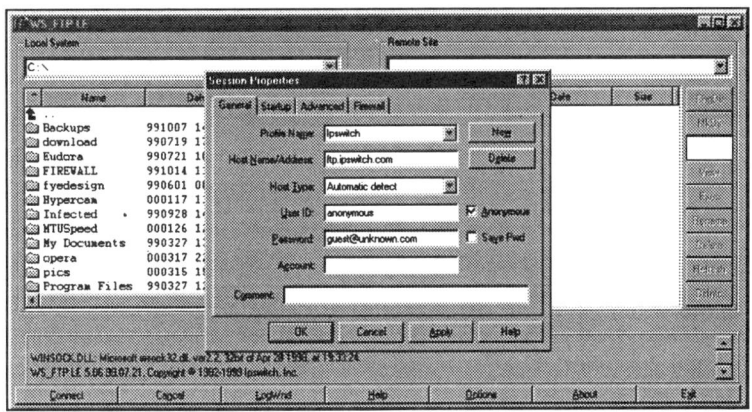

Using the details provided by your ISP, create a session profile for your site. By doing this you avoid the need to re-enter the details each time you upload files to your site. Click on the New button near the top of the Session Properties window to open a blank Session Properties window and enter the details required.

These include:

- **Profile Name:**
  Give your profile a name, such as "My website", for future reference. When you next run WS_FTP, select the profile name from the list of available profiles.

- **Host Name/Address:**
  Enter the Internet address of the Web server.

- **Host Type:**
  Leave this set to Automatic Detect.

- **User ID:**
  Your userid (or the userid that your ISP instructs you to use).

- **Password:**
  Your password (or the password your ISP gives you to use).

- **Account:**
  Leave this blank unless you are instructed to use a specific account by your ISP.

If you store your website files in a specific directory on your hard disk, or if you are required to upload files to a specific directory on your ISP's Web server, click the Startup tab and enter these details in the Initial Directories section. WS_FTP will use these default directories each time it starts. Check the checkbox labelled "Save Pwd" (password) and ensure the checkbox labelled "Anonymous" is unchecked. If the latter is checked this will cause WS_FTP to supply a generic password to the Web server, rather than your password, generating an error message.

If your ISP was "Big Pond", for example, your Session Properties might look like this:

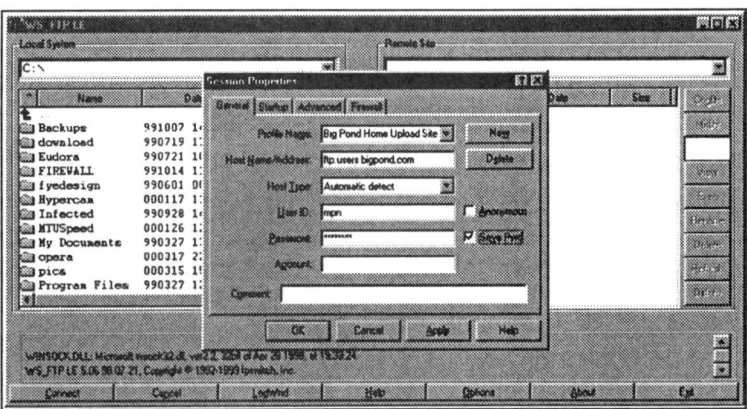

Connecting to the Web Server

Once you have entered your details, and checked for typographical errors, click on the OK button. WS_FTP will then attempt to connect to the Web server, and log in using the userid and password specified. If all goes well, it will display the contents of your Internet account.

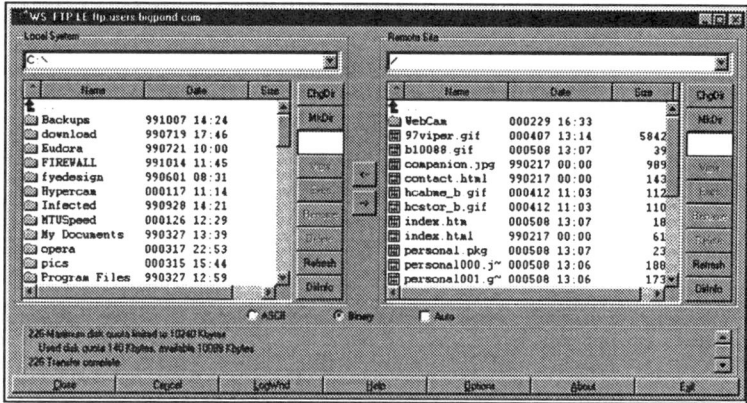

If you have problems connecting, go back and check your settings. If these are correct you may need to contact your ISP for help.

Once you have successfully connected to the Web server, the screen will be divided into two windows.

In the left-hand window (titled "Local System"), the contents of the default directory of your hard disk are displayed (generally the directory in which WS_FTP is installed, unless you specified otherwise in the Initial Directories option). In the right-hand window (titled "Remote Site"), the contents of your Internet account are displayed (below).

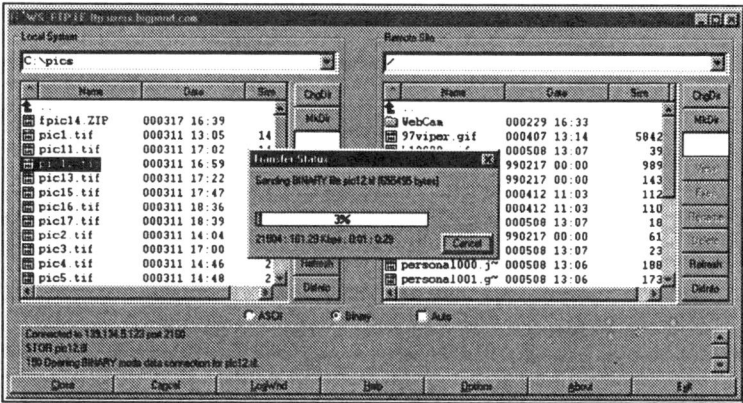

Uploading Files

Open the directory that contains your website files in the Local System window. To move from one directory on your hard disk to another click on the relevant drive letter (C: for most hard disks), then select the relevant directory from the list displayed.

Once you have opened the relevant directory in the Local System window, highlight a file that you wish to transfer by clicking on it once. Next, click on the arrow pointing to the Remote Site window (located on the pane between the two windows). WS_FTP will then copy the file to your Internet account (the original will still be on your computer). Unless it is a sizeable file (such as a graphic), it should be uploaded in a matter of seconds (below, left)!

Downloading files (that is, copying them from your Internet account to your computer) is achieved in the same way - simply highlight the name of a file displayed in the Remote System window, then click on the arrow pointing to the Local Site window.

A word of warning about filenames. Most Web servers use the Unix operating system. Unix is very case sensitive, unlike Windows and Macintosh computers. You must ensure that your filenames use upper and lower case in a uniform fashion. To a Unix Web server, index.html and Index.html are completely different files.

If your Web documents refer to a file, such as page2.html, then it must be named page2.html, not page2.HTML or Page2.html. This is one of the most common causes of problems when publishing Web documents. To avoid this problem, adopt a uniform method of naming files (for example, use lower case only).

Testing your Site

Even though you tested your website by viewing the files on your hard disk with a Web browser, it is a good idea to test the site again once it is uploaded and before you start publicising it. Check for a number of potential problems, including:

- How quickly your website loads. (There will be a marked difference between the time it takes to load from your hard disk, and the time required for the text and graphics to be downloaded and displayed from your Internet site.)
- Obvious errors (such as typographical mistakes).
- Missing or corrupt images.

Preview your website using at least both Internet Explorer and Netscape Navigator (these are the two most popular Web browsers), as your files can appear differently on each of these browsers. Although these differences are fairly minor, they can dramatically affect what visitors to your site see.

Another common problem is "missing" images. This can simply be due to a typographical error, such as referring to an image as "logo.jpg" when it is saved on the Web server as "Logo.jpg", which can cause difficulties for case-sensitive Web servers.

Make sure your pages contain the exact names that your files will use. In addition, ensure that your graphic and image files are in the same directory as the rest of your Web files. This is not a strict rule, as it is possible to organise files into specific directories, but beginners usually find it easier to troubleshoot when all the files are in the same place.

As you become more confident with Web designing, and develop more complex sites, you will find it is often convenient to separate files into different directories. For now, however, it's easiest to place all your files in the same directory.

Before you test your website, make sure you "flush" your Web browser's cache. Web browsers store copies of recently viewed websites in a special cache directory on your hard disk. If you revisit a website that is already stored in the cache, your Web browser will

Doctor HTML provides detailed results that will help
you pinpoint potential problems.

load the files from the cache (as this is faster than downloading the files again). When you view your website online, your browser might try to load the (now obsolete) files from its cache. If you don't want to flush the cache, you can ensure you are viewing the latest file by clicking on your Web browser's Reload button.

HTML validation Services

As a final measure before publicising your website, take advantage of one of the many HTML validation services.

These services have special programs that will visit your site and scan your documents for HTML errors. If they find problems that might cause difficulties when viewed with a specific browser, they will report back to you (usually via email) with a summary of the problem, and often a hint on how to remedy it. Some validation services even pick up spelling mistakes! (Beware of US sites that offer US-style spelling corrections.)

Some of the better HTML validators are:

Dr Watson	watson.addy.com
HTML Chek	uts.cc.utexas.edu/~churchh/htmlchek.html
Dr HTML	www2.imagiware.com/RxHTML/
Bobby	www.cast.org/bobby/
NetMechanic	www.netmechanic.com
website Garage	websitegarage.netscape.com

or for a list of checkers, go to:

www.flfsoft.com/html/html_validators.html

These services are really more for "peace of mind" than anything - modern Web authoring programs should check for "compliant" code. But it is better to be safe than sorry!

Resources

Free Web Hosting Services

A growing number of sites offer free Web hosting. Some are absolutely free of charge. Others, while still free, require you to display at least one banner ad on your site as provided by the hosting service.

Nearly all provide a very reasonable amount of space for hosting your site - at least 5Mb. Many also offer their users access to special website functions, including hit counters (so you know how many people have visited your site) and "visitor books" (which visitors can use to leave comments about your site). However, if you require advanced services, such as e-commerce functionality, you are unlikely to find a free service that meets your needs.

If your website budget is nil and your ISP can't help you out with Web hosting, try these free Web-hosting services.

Geocities	geocities.yahoo.com
Angelfire Communications	angelfire.lycos.com
50Megs	50megs.com
XOOM	www.xoom.com
Wow Sites	www.wowsites.com
WebJump	www.webjump.com

For a more exhaustive list of free Web-hosting services, see:

123FreePage	www.123freepage.com
Free Webpage list	Freeweblist.freeservers.com
FreeWebspace.Net	www.freewebspace.net

FTP Programs

Arnarchie (Mac)	www.stairways.com/anarchie/
Fetch (Mac)	www.dartmouth.edu/
Transmit (Mac)	www.panic.com
CuteFTP (Win)	www.cuteftp.com
WS_FTP (Win)	www.ipswitch.com/
3D FTP (Win)	www.3dftp.com
BulletProof FTP (Win)	www.bpftp.com
CoffeeCup Direct DFTP (Win)	www.coffeecup.com

For more information about FTP, including detailed, step-by-step tutorials, visit:

FTP Planet	www.ftpplanet.com

Chapter 10

Bandwidth Constraints

If there is one word you are guaranteed to hear, both as an Internet user and as a Web designer, it's bandwidth. The technical definition of bandwidth is "the maximum amount of data (text and images) that can be sent through a communications path in a given time (usually measured in megabytes per second, or Mbps)". Most users conceptualise bandwidth in terms of pipes - the wider the pipe (that is, the higher its bandwidth) the more data that can flow through it at once.

Bandwidth is a very important - and perplexing - issue, especially from a Web designer's perspective. If you don't grab your visitors' attention very soon after their arrival at your site, you run the risk that they will leave in search of more interesting sites. However, if your site is so complex, and its files so large, that it chokes the "pipe", it will take ages to load, increasing the chances that visitors will leave.

When it comes to online content, "interesting" usually equates to "bandwidth-intensive". Balancing interesting and visually stimulating content against bandwidth limitations can be a real dilemma. In this chapter, we will look at some strategies you can adopt to make the most of the available bandwidth.

Some Mathematics

While today's technologies allow high-speed Internet access at an affordable price, many Internet users access the Internet using older, slower technologies. As such, you should assume the average download speed achievable by your visitors is 3Kbps (that is, they can download 3 Kilobytes of data each second). Therefore, a 20Kb website logo (which is quite small compared to some graphics on websites today), would take roughly seven seconds to be downloaded and displayed on the user's screen (20 ÷ 3 = 6.66).

If your website contains a 20Kb logo, an animated email icon (15Kb), and four buttons (10Kb each) used as hyperlinks to other areas of your website, your opening page would contain 75Kb of graphics. This would take the average user 25 seconds to download - and we haven't yet included the text your Web page contains (although text downloads quite quickly, unless you have literally pages and pages of text in a single Web document).

Bandwidth Tricks

Unless your website offers content so compelling that users will want to wait for graphics to download, you

Hint

The speed a modem is rated at (such as 56Kbps) is not necessarily the speed at which users can download data. A number of variables affect "real world" download speeds, including how quickly the Web server repondes to requests and how congested the network is between the server and the user's ISP's network.

will maximise your chances of keeping their attention if you minimise your use of graphics.

This doesn't mean you have to forsake colour and multimedia on your website. But it does mean you have to work a little smarter. These tricks can let you have your cake and eat it too:

- **Offer visitors "high" and "low bandwidth" alternatives.**
  It doesn't take too much effort to create "mirror" copies of your website. One version can use large amounts of graphics and multimedia; the other should contain minimal graphics for those who are in a hurry or who don't want to wait for graphics to download.

- **Prefer the JPEG file format (.jpg) to GIF files (.gif) when saving custom-made graphics.**
  Images saved in JPEG format are generally smaller files, as this format has better data compression. However, it's not just a simple matter of saving all your images as JPEGs, as JPEG compression can affect image quality. In short, you'll need to experiment to obtain the best quality-to-size ratio.
  One solution is to use a graphics manipulation program to comp-ress image files (either by saving them with greater compression or by converting them from one graphics format to another, such as from GIF to JPEG). You'll find a number of

useful free or shareware graphics manipulation programs available on the Internet (as discussed in Chapter 4).

- **Reuse graphics on your website where possible.**
  Once a user's Web browser has downloaded an image, it is generally stored in a local "cache" on the user's hard disk. If the user revisits your website or accesses another area of your site that uses the same graphic, the Web browser will use the copy of the image stored in the cache, rather than re-download it. This speeds up the display of graphics considerably.

- **Use a reduced colour palette.**
  Most graphics programs work with colour palettes, which determine the number of colours that can be used within a specific image.
  GIF images, for example, generally use an 8-bit palette, with the result that up to 256 colours can be used within a single image. Most Web graphics, however, use fewer than four or eight colours. By reducing the number of colours available in the palette used to create an image, you can achieve considerable savings in file sizes.
  For example, by using a 6-bit palette, you will still have access to 64 colours, but reduce your file sizes by around 25 per cent. Your graphic program's help menu should provide instructions on how to reduce the colour palette.

- **If you are determined to use a background image, use a very small one.**
  If the background image is used primarily to create a custom background colour, create only very small images (for example, 4 x 72 pixels). The Web browser will "tile" the image (that is, repeat it over and over again, filling the screen background).
  Also, there is no need to "interlace" background images, as this will add unnecessarily to the file's size. Interlacing is handy for displaying larger images, but it is wasted on small, background images.
  Unless you have a specific need for a custom background image, use the <BODY BGCOLOR="xxxxxx"> tag (see Chapter

6) to set the background colour, where "xxxxxx" is one of the standard HTML colour names.

- **Save images at low resolution.**
  The lower you set your image resolution, the smaller the resulting file will be. Unless you have a compelling need to publish images at high resolution (for example, if you are selling art online), don't save your images at anything higher than 72dpi.

Resources

Bandwidth Conservation Soc.	www.infohiway.com/faster/
Web page budgeting	www.dreamink.com/speed3.html
JPEG FAQ File	www.faqs.org/faqs/jpeg-faq

The Bandwidth Conservation Society
offers helpful tips for trimming your Web pages

Chapter 11

Promoting Your Website

It used to be that the simple act of publishing a website effectively guaranteed an audience. In the Internet's early years there were few websites around, and those that did exist were fairly dry affairs used to disseminate scientific data. Today, users are overwhelmed by choice, and competition is fierce. If you want people to visit your site, you have to work hard to make it stand out from the crowd.

The Eyes Have It

When the Web first began, users kept written lists of their favourite sites, or memorised the addresses of sites they used regularly. Today, maintaining a list of favourite sites by hand would be a full-time job in itself. Memorising them would be next to impossible!

Search Engines were created to solve these problems. Search Engines, such as Yahoo! (www.yahoo.com) and AltaVista (www.altavista.com), are essentially massive indexes of websites.

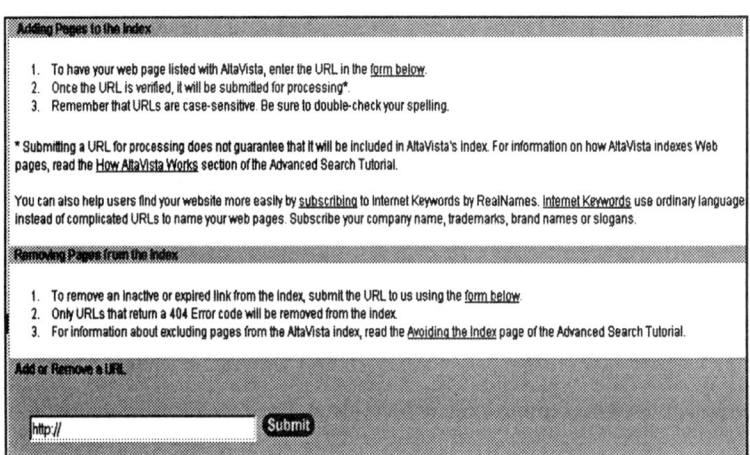

AltaVista allows any user to submit their Web site's details for indexing

Web robots are sent out on behalf of Search Engines to scan the Internet all day every day for new websites. As new sites are found, their contents are indexed and the details stored in the Search Engines' databases. Users can locate websites of interest by performing key-word searches of these databases. As such, Search Engines play an integral role in site-promotion. In fact, unless you have unlimited funds to promote your website using traditional advertising methods, listing your site with Search Engines can mean the difference between anonymity and celebrity!

Spreading the Word

Registering your website with a Search Engine (or several) involves visiting each Search Engine's site and following the prompts to complete the submission process. Most of the major websites have a button marked "Add URL" (or something similar) or a link on their home page. "URL" stands for "uniform resource locator" - that is, the address of a website.

Search Engines generally use one of two methods for accepting additions to their databases. The first method is to prompt you for the URL of the website to be added to the database. The Search Engine's Web robot then visits the site, indexes its contents and adds this to the Search Engine's database. AltaVista is an example of a Search Engine that adopts this method. Other Search Engines expect the user to do most of the "leg work", requiring all the necessary information about the site (such as who owns/maintains it, what type or category of information it contains) plus a short summary that tells potential visitors what the site contains. Yahoo! is one of several Search Engines that use this method.

Directories

Web directories play much the same role as Search Engines. Directories generally maintain listings of sites related to one or more topics. Most are "single topic", which means they only list sites related to a single topic. Some of the more advanced directories also offer limited search functions.

Web directories are an excellent place to list your website, as you can be sure that their users are looking for fairly specific information or products. For a list of available Web directories, check out the Resources section at the end of this chapter.

Submission Services

It really pays to spend some time registering your website with Search Engines and directories. But accessing each Search Engine and registering your website can be tedious. Thankfully, a number of websites offer automated promotion services. Simply supply the details of your site, and these sites will automatically submit its details to several Search Engines and directories.

Services of this nature can be a real blessing, especially if you want to get the word out quickly about your website. However, there are a few catches. While the automated submission services are generally free, the sites are usually operated by professional Web marketing companies, who use these free services as a marketing tool for their other services. In fact, some of the sites are little more than an advertisement for the pay-per-use services.

Other services may submit your site to only a limited number of Search Engines. For example, SubmitIt! will register your website with a number of popular Search Engines free of charge, but also offers fee-based services that will register your website with up to 400 Search Engines, directories and other promotional vehicles. Your best bet, therefore, is to use several different free prom-otional services. Once you have registered your website with a variety of Search Engines, directories, and other promotional websites, check how your listings are working. You can do this using the services offered by PositionAgent (www.positionagent.com).

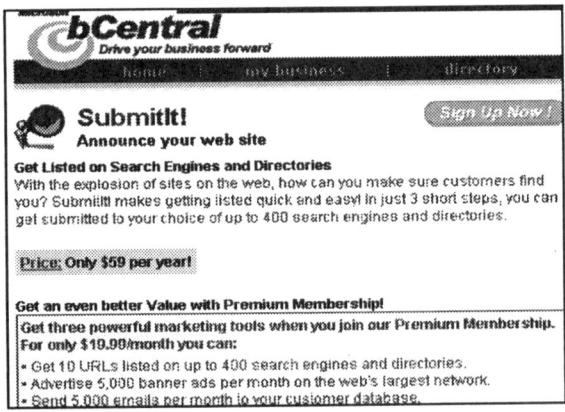

The SubmitIt! promotion Website at www.submitit.com

is an excellent resource for promoting your Web site

Meta Tags

Meta tags are a neat "trick" that can help you promote your site. Most Search Engines and directories support the use of meta tags, which operate as a helpful hint for Search Engines and other online catalogues and directories.

The tags are essentially a collection of keywords that describe your website and the contents and resources it offers. Search Engines can use these as guides when determining how to index and categorise your website. The most popular meta tags are the description and keyword tags. The content of the description meta tag is displayed by meta tag-enabled Search Engines when listing your site in search results.

The contents of the keyword meta tag are used by Search Engines as part of their categorising process. Instead of sifting through the text of your website trying to pick appropriate key words, meta tag-enabled Search Engines will index your website according to the key words you supply. Use as many key words as you think appropriate, but try to keep the number of characters to between 150 and 200 (including spaces) and don't repeat keywords, as most Search Engines will ignore repetitive key words.

When selecting your key words, make sure you are describing your website rather than your company. Users searching for information or products of interest will be disappointed if, after hunting for information and being directed to your website, it does not offer the promised information.

For example, if your company offers com-puter training in all popular Windows programs, but your website only contains information on Excel, limit your meta-tags to Excel. Meta tags should appear between the <HEAD> tags in your Web documents (for more information on HTML tags, see Chapter 6).

Meta tags are used as follows:

```
<HEAD>
<TITLE>Title</TITLE>
<META Name="description" Content="Write your
description here">
<METAName="key    words"    Content="Write    your
keywords here">
</HEAD>
```

If you're not sure which meta tags to use for your site, don't worry, as there are programs that will prepare them for you. See the resources list at the end of this chapter for pointers to these sites.

Banners

Another form of effective promotion is the use of banners. We discussed in Chapter 4 how banners can be used to advertise the contents of your site to visitors. But you can also use banners to attract visitors from other websites.

There are generally three ways you can achieve this. The first is to pay for advertising space on popular websites, such as Yahoo! or CNet (www.cnet.com). However, for most website owners, this option is too expensive. The second alternative is to enter into a banner exchange agreement with one or several friendly website owners. Basically, you agree to include their banner on your website in exchange for the inclusion of your banner on theirs. This can be especially useful if you partner with sites that contain information or services similar to yours. For example, if yours is a hobby website discussing scuba diving, you might swap banners with other scuba enthusiasts' sites. Similarly, if your website sells fitness equipment, you might swap banners with a fitness-related website.

The third alternative is to join one of a number of professionally organised "banner exchange" services. These generally require you to register your website with the co-ordinating site and supply a copy of your banner, which is added to a database of available banners. In return for access to this service - which is free - you must agree to display the banners of other banner exchange members on your website. Often you are given some special HTML code to insert on your Web pages to do this.

Once you modify your website with the special code, a banner from another banner exchange member will be displayed on your website. But instead of displaying one, static banner, a new banner is displayed each time a visitor visits your site.

Each time a banner is displayed to a visitor to your website, you receive a "credit". The banner exchange's computers track these credits and the number of credits earned by your site dictate both the number of sites that display your banners and the frequency with which they are displayed. Such services can be both easy to implement and beneficial to all participants.

There are many different banner exchange programs. You'll find pointers to a few in the resources section below.

Resources

Web Search Engines
For an exhaustive list of Web Search engines, check Yahoo!'s listing at:
www.yahoo.com.au/Computers_and_Internet/Internet/World_Wide_Web/Searching_the_Web/Search_Engines/

Web directories
For an exhaustive list of Web directories, check Yahoo!'s listing at:
www.yahoo.com.au/Computers_and_Internet/Internet/World_Wide_Web/Searching_the_Web/Search_Engines/Web_Directories/

Promotion services
The following websites offer free (and, in some cases, very effective) submission website services:

SubmitIt!	www.submitit.com
@Submit	www.uswebsites.com/submit/
Add Me	www.addme.com
Register-It	www.register-it.com
Did-It	www.did-it.com
Link Popularity	www.linkpopularity.com
Site Owner	siteowner.linkexchange.com
Net Mechanic	www.netmechanic.com

For a more comprehensive list, visit Yahoo!'s list at:
www.yahoo.com.au/Business_and_Economy/Companies/Internet_Services/Web_Services/Promotion

Promotion Software
Some of these programs are free, while others are pay-per-use. All will save you time and hassles.

Web Position Gold	www.webposition.com
TopDogg	http://www.topdogg.com/
SubmitWolf	www.trellian.com
Site Promoter	www.sitepromoter.com

Meta Tag Generators

Meta Tag Builder

vancouver-webpages.com/
VWbot/mk-metas.html

Meta Tag Generator

www.websitepromote.com/
resources/meta/

Banner Exchange

Banner Swap   www.bannerswap.com
Better Deals   www.betterdeals.com
Internet Link Exchange   www.linkexchange.com

For a more extensive list of banner exchange programs, visit:
www.yahoo.com.au/Computers_and_Internet/Internet/World_Wide
_Web/Announcement_Services/Banner_Exchanges/

Chapter 12

Websites that WOW!

SuperGoals
www.supergoals.com

SuperGoals, launched by the same company that publishes The Sun, appears to have a simple "goal" (if you'll pardon the pun) - to be a one-stop news resource for football fanatics. Site navigation is aided by a straight-forward navigation menu displayed down the left side of the screen, allowing visitors to jump directly to the soccer sections of interest to them.

The balance of the homepage is taken up by short, punchy, hyperlinked news headlines. Graphic usage is limited, and the text and headlines are well spaced, with plenty of white background making for an easy reading layout.

Burgled
www.burgled.com

This site is a prime example of good intentions but poor execution. Burgled.com is a fairly useful resource for those who find their homes burgled (or who wish to avoid being burgled). It is predominantly text-based with high-contrast colours, so it loads very quickly and is easy to read on-screen.

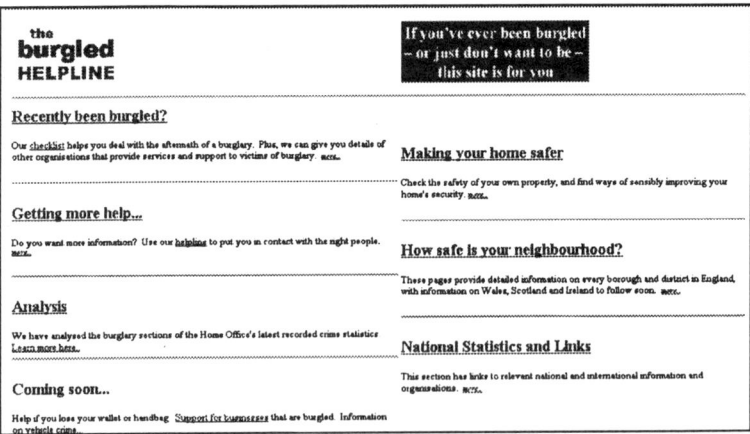

Unfortunately, the layout looks very chaotic, and the homepage lacks a dominant element, with the result that new visitors could quite easily become confused as to where they should head next. Worst of all, the homepage looks so cluttered visitors might be inclined to leave without even trying to understand the site.

Untitled Document
www.untitleddocument.co.uk

Untitled Document is a tongue-in-cheek look at the stories making headlines around the world (plus some made up stuff thrown in for good measure). The layout is very compact and simple. The homepage features a handful of navigation links, which appear to the top, left of the screen; and links to the day's main stories at the top middle of the screen, with several story excerpts occupying the remainder of the page.

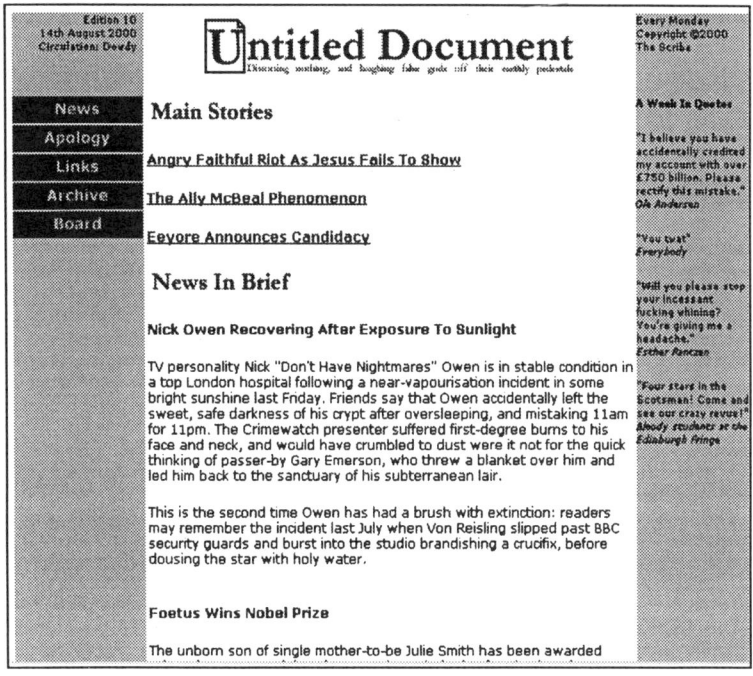

Graphics have been kept to a minimum, as is the use of colour. The grey and black on a white background offers high contrast, with hyperlinks left in their default blue to ensure there is no confusion among new users.

MTV2
www.mtv2.co.uk

As you would expect from the team behind MTV, this is a very slick Web site. Using the latest version of Flash, the Web site seems to do its best *not* to look like a Web site.

Each screen features a single, animated, interactive graphic which displays navigation options as you slide your mouse over on-screen graphic elements.

While the site can be slow to load in parts (because of the graphic overhead), it quickly becomes quite intuitive, which is surprising given the scant navigational cues and lack of "depth"

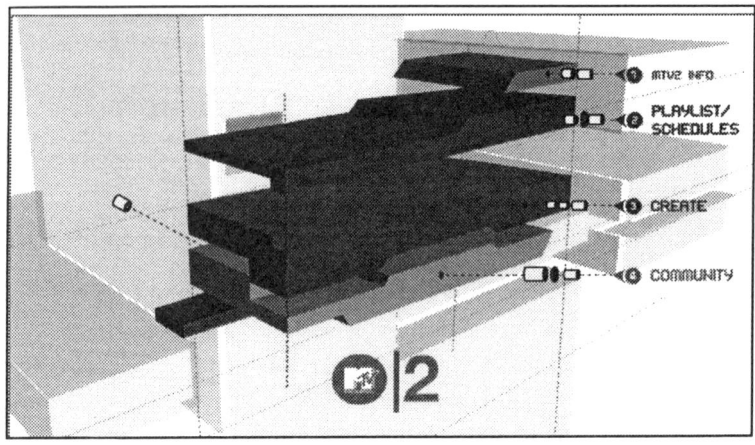

perception (there are few clues to indicate where on the site you are, what bits you haven't seen and where you should visit next).

Urban Fetch
www.urbanfetch.co.uk

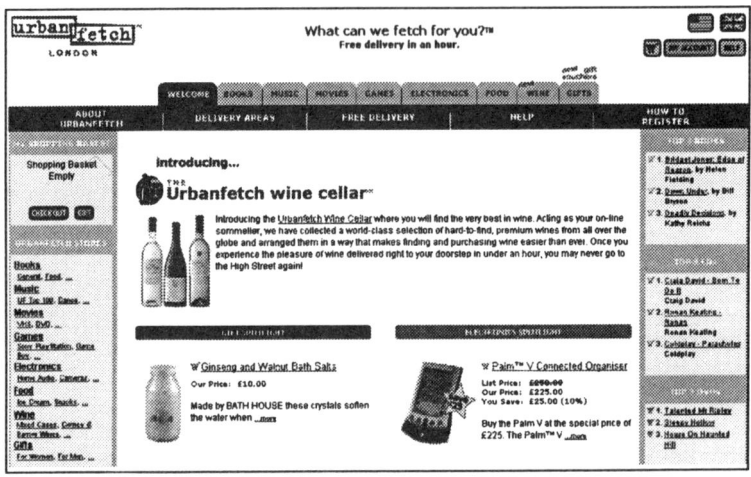

UrbanFetch is an online shopping service promising free home delivery within an hour for a wide variety of products. If you have ever visited the Amazon.com Web site, you will soon notice that UrbanFetch has "borrowed" heavily from Amazon.com's design principles. Although this costs the site in terms of originality, it wins bonus points in terms of user-friendliness.

The site features a range of "tabs" across the top of the screen, allowing shoppers to jump directly to the product category of interest to them. The left side of the screen is dominated by a category-style summary of the site's offerings, and the right side features a list of recommended purchases etc. The layout is neat, well organised and approachable.

TubeHell
www.tubehell.com

TubeHell is one of those sites which initially sounds like a bit of a flash-in-the-pan, but the more you think of it, the more it grows on you. The Web site seeks to create a virtual community around the shared "hell" created for daily commuters by London's underground train system. The central navigation element is a witty play on standard train system maps, with each menu option representing a station on the map. Layout is quite uniform, and navigation elements appear in predictable places, which makes for a user-friendly experience. The only real complaint is the use of orange text on a deep red background, which may not be very readable for those with poor vision.

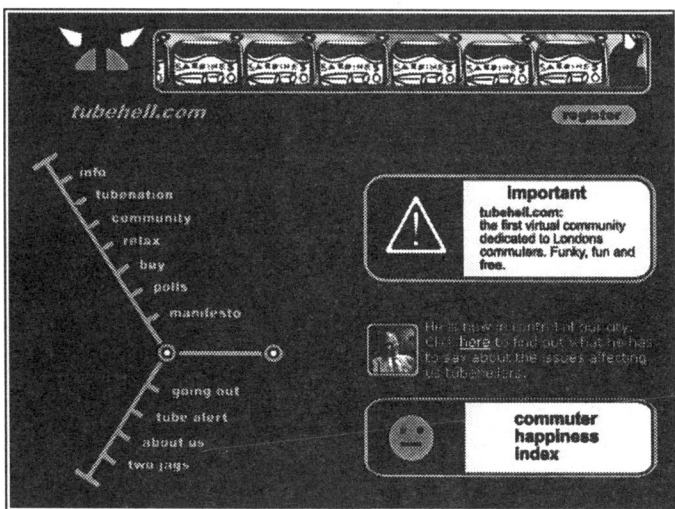

The Net-Works Guide to
Marketing Your Website

Simply creating a website and putting it on the Internet is not enough to generate online sales, no matter how good it looks. In Cyberspace there simply isn't any passing traffic. The customer is king, and they will selectively choose which sites they are going to visit. Indeed, without a well thought-out and successfully implemented marketing plan, the majority of your potential customers will not even know that you are out there.

What is more, even if you have a few years of 'real life' marketing experience under your belt, you have a lot to learn, and unlearn, before attempting to market your website. The Internet is a very different medium from those you may be used to, and your marketing strategy will have to adapt accordingly if you want to enjoy any kind of success.

Online Marketing Made Easy

The Net-Works Guide to Marketing Your Website will show you how to construct and deliver a successful promotional strategy. It covers everything from the basics of linking to other sites and search engine registration, through to referral sales and associate programs. No stone is left unturned in the quest for more visitors. You will learn:

● How to promote your site in newsgroups and chat rooms without being flamed,
● The importance of META tags and how to use them,
● How to build customer loyalty,
● What is meant by 'sticky content' and how to write it,
● Why e-zines, newsletters and bait pages are important,
● Ways of promoting your site in the traditional media,

Anyone reading this book, and putting its easy-to-follow, non-technical advice into operation, can expect a rapid increase in the number of hits to their website.

Tim Ireland   112 pages   £7.95

Starting and Running a Business on the Internet

Do you want to:

✔ Sell your goods all over the world without leaving your office chair?
✔ Tap the fastest growing and most affluent market ever?
✔ Slash your marketing and advertising costs?
✔ Talk to the other side of the world for free?
✔ Have access to strategic information only the biggest companies could afford?

Then your business should be on the Internet!

Companies are already cutting costs, improving customer support and reaching hitherto untapped markets via the Internet. They have realised the potential for this exciting new commercial arena and they've grabbed the opportunity with both hands. Now you can join in the fun of what is still a 'ground floor' opportunity.

Starting and Running a Business on The Internet offers realistic and practical advice for any existing business or budding 'Cyberpreneur'. It also:

❏ Helps you get started QUICKLY and CHEAPLY.
❏ Tells you which sites 'work', which don't and, more importantly, WHY!
❏ Details how to PROMOTE your business online.
❏ Shows you how to stay ahead of your competitors.
❏ Warns you of the major PITFALLS and shows you how to AVOID them.
❏ Highlights important issues like CREDIT CARD handling and site SECURITY.

Alex Kiam   112 pages   £6.95

Book Ordering

To order any of these books, please order from our secure website at **www.net-works.co.uk** or complete the form below (or use a plain piece of paper) and send to:

Europe/Asia
TTL, PO Box 200, Harrogate HG1 2YR, England (or fax to 01423-526035, or email: sales@net-works.co.uk).

USA/Canada
Trafalgar Square, PO Box 257, Howe Hill Road, North Pomfret, Vermont 05053 (or fax to 802-457-1913, call toll free 800-423-4525, or email: tsquare@sover.net)

Postage and handling charge:
UK - £1 for first book, and 50p for each additional book
USA - $5 for first book, and $2 for each additional book (all shipments by UPS, please provide street address).
Elsewhere - £3 for first book, and £1.50 for each additional book (for courier rates, please fax or email for a price quote)

Book	Qty	Price
	Postage	
	Total:	

☐ I enclose payment for £_____

☐ Please debit my VISA/AMEX/MASTERCARD

Number: ☐☐☐☐ ☐☐☐☐ ☐☐☐☐ ☐☐☐☐

Expiry Date: ☐☐☐☐ Signature: Date:

Name: _____

Address: _____

_____

_____

Postcode/Zip:_____

Telephone/Email:_____

wow